PENGUIN BOOKS

SECRETS OF A VERY GOOD MARRIAGE

Sherry Suib Cohen is a free-lance writer whose articles appear regularly in such newspapers and magazines as *The New York Times, Glamour, Mademoiselle, Ladies' Home Journal,* and *New Woman,* where she is a contributing editor. She is the author of *The Magic of Touch* and *Tender Power,* among others. She lives in New York City.

Sherry Suib Cohen

SECRETS OF A VERY GOOD MARRIAGE

LESSONS FROM THE SEA

PENGUIN BOOKS

PENGUIN BOOKS
Published by the Penguin Group
Penguin Books USA Inc., 375 Hudson Street,
New York, New York 10014, U.S.A.
Penguin Books Ltd, 27 Wrights Lane, London W8 5TZ, England
Penguin Books Australia Ltd, Ringwood, Victoria, Australia
Penguin Books Canada Ltd, 10 Alcorn Avenue, Toronto,
Ontario, Canada M4V 3B2
Penguin Books (N.Z.) Ltd, 182–190 Wairau Road,
Auckland 10, New Zealand

Penguin Books Ltd, Registered Offices:
Harmondsworth, Middlesex, England

First published in the United States of America
by Carol Southern Books 1993
Reprinted by arrangement with Clarkson N. Potter, Inc.
Published in Penguin Books 1994

3 5 7 9 10 8 6 4 2

THE LIBRARY OF CONGRESS HAS CATALOGUED THE HARDCOVER AS FOLLOWS:
Cohen, Sherry Suib.
Secrets of a very good marriage: lessons from the sea/Sherry Suib Cohen.
ISBN 0-517-58947-8 (hc.)
ISBN 0 14 02.3877 8 (pbk.)
1. Marriage.   2. Man–woman relationships.   3. Ocean.   4. Fishing.   I. Title.
HQ801.C64   1993
646.7'8—dc20   92–44277

Printed in the United States of America
Set in Aldus
Designed by Barbara deWilde

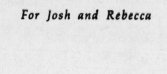

For Josh and Rebecca

GRATEFUL THANKS TO

Connie Clausen, who saw it.
Carol Southern, who carved and shaped it.
Susan, Adam, Jennifer, Steven, Jane, and David—the fleet.
Larry, my mate.

CONTENTS

PROLOGUE   xiii

PART 1 :
LAUNCHINGS

1. MY FIRST TIME   3
2. HUE   6
3. NO MULLET FISHING   10
4. A GOOD BOAT   13
5. YOU HAVE TO HAVE BEEN THERE   16
6. RITUAL, SEA, AND EARTH   20
7. NAMING   23

PART 2 : TIDES

8. QUENELLES IN THE MACKEREL   29
9. AUDIBLE STROKES   34
10. COMMUNITY OF TWO   37
11. PATIENCE   41
12. TUNA ODYSSEY: THE GREAT
    GIVE-BACK   46
13. FIDELITY   52
14. BLUE WATER   56
15. CREATING INTIMACY   62

PART 3: CROSSCURRENTS

16. LANDMARKS   67
17. DANGER   71
18. GOING TOO FAR   75
19. WHERE HOME IS   79
20. NO ONE'S PERFECT   83
21. CHANGING THE SUBJECT   88
22. KNOTS   91
23. WEATHERING THE STORMS   96
24. SURRENDER   99

PART 4: SEA OF PLENTY

25. RENEWAL   105
26. LIFESAVERS   109
27. SO, WHAT DO YOU THINK?   114
28. FLIRTING   117
29. JUST DO IT   121
30. THE RICHLY LAYERED MARRIAGE   124
31. PASSION   130

THE SECRETS   **135**

My beloved may catch me with a Hook.

> *Hafiz, fourteenth-century Persian poet*

Sir Henry Wotton was a most dear lover and a frequent practiser of The Art Of Angling; of which he would say,

" 'Twas an employment for his idle time, which was then, not idly spent, a rest of his mind, a cheerer of his spirits, a diverter of sadness, a calmer of unquiet thoughts, a moderator of passions, a procurer of contentedness": and that it begat habits of peace and patience in those that professed and practised it."

> Izaak Walton, The Compleat Angler

. . . the honey of Sea-love delight.

> *Guillaume de Salluste du Bartas*
> *(1579)*

Come live with mee, and bee my love,
And wee will some new pleasures prove
Of golden sands and christall brookes
With silken lines, and silver hookes.
> *John Donne*

Fishing is complicated.
> *John Hersey,* Blues

PROLOGUE

Some remarkable karma has led me to draw a very happy marriage. In my heart of hearts I've always believed that this has happened not because I had smarts, but because I lucked out and found a sweet man who instinctively knew how to gentle me and the children when, left to our own devices, we'd rip out each other's throats. He's darling and funny and wise, and he says, "You're more beautiful than ever before, and you do *not* have neck sag" ten times a day. Sure, he can be astonishingly, Mr. Magoo–ishly forgetful and dazzlingly sloppy, but when a man values you, who cares if you trip over his shoes?

Together we are Elizabeth Barrett and Robert Browning, Mike Nichols and Elaine May, the Wright Brothers, Damon and Pythias, best friends, indestructible. We can't stop touching each other. It's been over thirty years. Our kids, all grown now, certainly like him best. Who could blame them? He never gives anyone grief. I like him best, too. So, until recently, I really thought *he* was the formula for our perfect marriage. I mean, I'm not exactly chopped liver, but he's a very nice person.

But, you know what? It takes two. I've come to understand that I also have something to do with the

way our years unfold so gracefully, so lovingly. I
mean—there's just certain stuff I *do*.

Most of the time, I kept my thoughts, kept our
ways, to myself. But secretly I'd wonder—how come
friends with troubled marriages couldn't have what we
had? How come everybody didn't know what we knew?

Then, over the years, it became increasingly apparent
that other great marriages we've heard of share certain
disciplines with our own marriage: call them secrets, call it
learned self-control. I am now convinced that there is
particular *behavior* that is at the matrix of tenderness.

Because I'm a writer, it's crossed my mind before to
share the secrets of our swell marriage, but, until now, I
never have. I don't even know if our way would work for
anyone else: how can I honestly say, "Do what we do
and your significant other will love only you, you'll have
great sex, be able to communicate, and share the deepest
passions"?

But then I decided:

I do want to write about it. No magic, no
lectures—just tell about the good we give to each other.
And how we give it to each other. And how this good
seems to flow from an astonishing source.

Because, here it comes. Besides being really terrific,
my husband is a wild-eyed fanatic, a pain in the ass about
one thing. He's a pain in the ass about fishing. He's loony
over the deep, down, wild sea. He's zany over salt air.
He's a lunkhead over ground-up-fish-head bait. Goes
absolutely bonkers when a stupid, ugly flounder bites.
Loves me, *worships* boat.

From the very start of our togetherness, he's longed

for me to worship the boat also. Worship? There are times when I loathe it, when I'm jealous of it, when I want to kick it, sink it. Because I love him, though, I've allowed myself to be shanghaied almost every weekend in fishing season. I've tried hard to understand the mentality of the boating man. This is difficult.

So, I never considered, not even for one minute, that boating—his obsession, what I once considered my involuntary servitude—had much to do with the quality of our marriage, but lately there are strong, clear clues to our sweet union that have been puffing out, like skywriting at the beach. How come I never noticed them before? Maybe I haven't looked up. Or, more accurately, down—at the sensational, heaving, sage sea. The fact is, unbelievable as I still find it, almost everything good I've learned about marriage and love and family have come from the sea. The lessons of the sea.

When, after a long day, we leave the boat (cunningly called the *Sherry J.* to appease me), I see him secretly, slowly, run his hand along its flanks—more sensuously than he ever caressed mine—or at least *as* sensuously. For over thirty years I have been at his side as we battled the brave, giant tuna, the elements, and the throat-clutching charges of boatyard mechanics who hold his life's blood and my Porsche convertible in their tangled tool chests. He's loved it all.

I've loved about 39 percent of it all. Most of the time, I doze and dream on the roughly appointed (you have to lift up a cushion to get to the smelly head) wooden boat he canonizes, rousing myself to loud panic only when a brutal wind comes up or to cheer when

the scream of the reel announces a hookup. I try to
be stoic about the endless battering of the waves,
and uncomplaining as I wait for death or deliverance,
whichever comes first. That's not exactly true: I complain
bitterly starting about three in the afternoon. I complain
nonstop.

Mostly, Larry ignores me.

If I had *my* summer druthers, I'd be climbing the
green hillocks of Ireland, *not* fighting the brave, giant
tuna. I mean, I don't really give a damn about the brave,
giant tuna—only that it shouldn't bleed all over the boat.

So, here's the astounding part: The boat can be
boring and sometimes scary, but being a partner with the
sea, waiting for the giant tuna to bite, waiting for the tide
to turn, has taught me patience and bravery. And recently
I've had a true epiphany: Much of the patience, the pluck,
the excitement, the restraint, Larry's wisdom, our
combined strength, the way we *do*, has at its core the sea,
the wooden boat, the challenge, the passion—yes, I'll say
it—the eroticism of the sea and its dangers, the smell of
victory, the tedium, and, God help me, fishing itself. This,
I might add, doesn't stop me from kicking and screaming
in the cold, dark mornings when Larry kisses me awake
and says it's time to go fishing.

Nevertheless, it's become increasingly clear that the
peace in our home and in our hearts has a lot to do with
what we've learned on the water, where Larry has taught
me to fish for our lives, you might say.

PART 1 LAUNCHINGS

Learning How to Float

MY

FIRST TIME

Reach back into the memory of your first date
together and recapture the way you felt.
Do it often.

Decades after our marriage, we're still impelled to reminisce about our beginnings. They are a touchstone, the currency of our lives together. The time your hat blew off, the time I wouldn't go to Mexico with you because I had a dentist's appointment, your tiny basement apartment, when you yelled at me the first time we went out on the boat. . . .

So, this is the way it started: He was a blind date, and we met under the clock at the old Biltmore Hotel in New York and went to hear live jazz (my first time). I thought he was interesting in his rumpled tweed, and I liked the way the Dixieland musicians in the crowded, dark club greeted him with familiarity (not his first time). He took me to a restaurant after the music, and when he said he wasn't hungry and only wanted some crackers with his beer, I said I couldn't eat a thing, either, although I could have eaten a whole sheep. In those days girls didn't admit to appetites. Did I want to go fishing on his boat before the dawn broke the next morning? he asked. Sure I did. It would be my first time. *Quel* romantic.

Later, my mother leaped for joy. A boat? A *rich* young man. She strongly suggested I wear my white piqué sundress with my ribboned straw hat. Even in retrospect I can't blame her because I kind of liked the image myself. I'd been reading a lot of F. Scott Fitzgerald, and I visualized Larry at daybreak in these white bucks and white flannels and me, Daisy, in the piqué. The boat would be, well, a cross between the *Queen Elizabeth* and the *African Queen*.

Larry showed up at my door in the same rumpled tweed jacket he'd worn the night before, and the *Queen Elizabeth* was a rowboat. I don't think he noticed the piqué. He was innocent of my expectations, so excited, so loving, and on the long drive to the marina, he tried to explain what fishing and the sea meant to him. It all sounded heroic, poetic. Red sea at night, sailor's delight, red sky at morning, sailors take warning, that kind of thing. He wanted to show me what he loved—his picturesque, salmon-colored craft with its finely polished oars, the wriggling, silvery killie fish we would use as bait, the wooden bait box carefully tied to the bow, the way the tangerine sun burst over the horizon, the way he rowed the five miles to the open ocean—wasn't he captain of the crew in college? What muscles, what form! I murmured admiration for both. He ate it up.

Sweat poured down the rower's brow: it looked masculine. The tide was going out, the seawater was not exactly infused with Baccarat clarity, being a mass of moss and jellyfish and discarded Coke bottles with no messages. Still, I was acutely aware that I was making a memory, that the nuances of this early morning would color my life forever. I was a dream in white piqué. I knew how ethereal I looked. Finally, after an hour's hard row, we got to where the fish were. Larry asked me to open the hinged flap on the wooden killie box while he set the anchor. I leaned over to the sea's surface where the killie box floated and delicately opened its clever trap door. The killies swam out.

And then, on only our second date, and how was I to know it—the first and last time he'd ever yell at me—Larry yelled at me.

God damn it—in *the boat, you pull the box* in *the boat before you open it! Oh. Damn it.*

He rowed five miles back to get more bait. Apologized for yelling. But I was still miffed beyond words. How was I supposed to know? It was my first time.

———

Several months later, in love with the fisherman, I sat down under a tree in the schoolyard where I taught to consider his marriage proposal. By then I had a more realistic idea of what part fishing and hours and hours and hours and hours upon a painted sea and going to boat shows and polishing teak and baiting hooks with unspeakable objects would play in my future with this nice man. Oh, sure, he also loved books and travel, and he made me laugh, but could I take his obsession? Could I deal with this fishing? Would it get any better than the first time?

HUE

*Love has only one sure route: unconditional support,
even if you're scared, even if
you have to bluff it.*

We were on our honeymoon, it was the third blissful day, and we were out fishing the Bermuda waters. What else would we be doing? The wedding had been good: I'd looked down the length of the nine-mile-long aisle, seen Larry, waiting and smiling, and that smile had propelled me to him, fearlessly. Later, that night, I wasn't so fearless. I'd put on my virginal, miles-of-diaphanous nightgown/uniform and felt like a jerk. Also, *very* virginal, inept, inexperienced, doltish, embarrassed. Would I have to take it off? Couldn't it all be in the dark? It could and it was, and my young husband was a tender teacher. We loved for hours and then we whispered our good-nights.

Three in the morning I was still excruciatingly wide awake, stiff-necked, Larry's arm lovingly around me. He, on the other hand, slept as if he'd never left his boyhood bunk bed, as if this weren't his wedding night. Men. My immediate problem was that it appeared I couldn't sleep with *anyone's* arm wedged under my neck, new husband or not.

Was I doomed to spend the rest of my life sleepless because I could never tell him to remove that arm? How unromantic, how ungrateful, that would be. I silently and carefully got out of bed and stared at the misty rain from the hotel window, suddenly sunk in a peculiar, nameless depression. He sensed me gone, woke, came to hold me, and suggested we dress and take a walk. At four A.M.? said my mother's daughter. Why not? he said. It was, somehow, exactly the right thing to do—a surrealistic touch to a surrealistic night: the walk felt exhilarating, crazy—I looked at other night owls passing by and soundlessly shouted to them, "I just did it—for the first time!" I was sure I looked different.

Then I told Larry about the arm problem. He laughed and promised I wouldn't have to be forever sleepless.

So, three days later, we were on a boat and happy in Bermuda. When he told me we would be fishing for dolphin, I felt sick. Dolphin? Flipper? I'd married a monster. No, he said patiently, not that kind of dolphin, that's a mammal. Do you think I would fish for Flipper?

It was almost as bad, though, because when you caught the phosphorescent, gorgeously blue-green-yellow creature, its colors began to fade almost as soon as it was boated. I couldn't believe it: brilliant blue turned to ashes before my eyes. Cobalt to leaden gray. When the fish finally died, it was a different being—a mouse-colored, dull thing.

It was as if the spirit of the fish had hue; when the spirit died, the hue was gone.

The Roman philosopher Seneca acidly described one of Nero's banquets, where between the lavish courses a mullet was passed around the table, flapping frantically in a waterless bowl; Nero's dinner guests could thus entertain themselves with the sight of its gorgeous yellows and reds going flat as the mullet fluttered toward death. I reminded Larry of this story. He was not grateful but took the opportunity to tell me that I must learn not to identify with the fish.

"The fish we catch is food, and we are only acting as part of the giant food chain," he instructed me. "I promise you we'll never kill anything we won't eat."

Oh, okay. I'd try.

———

Later that night we lay together for only the fourth time in our honeymoon bed, and Larry, who wanted to love me, couldn't. We hugged each other and told each other how happy we were, but nothing worked.

Frankly, I was scared. Innocent when I married, I had never heard of this. Was I doing something wrong? Was he not attracted to me? Was there something terribly wrong with *him?*

Larry was grim and silent. He was more experienced than I, but barely, and this was a new thing for him. And on his *honeymoon:* he was mortified and terrified. He turned pale.

Imagination racing, a vision of the afternoon's dolphin flashed in my head. A dying spirit. Pale. Impaled.

From I don't know where, smart words started coming from my frightened mouth. To this day, I can't believe that I didn't whine with terror, blame, defend myself—all as natural as breathing for me. Somehow I knew exactly what I had to do, which was to smother my fear and bolster his strength. This is *nothing*, I assured my young husband. *Nothing.* Believe me. You are trying too hard. You want it to be perfect. You have never been in love before—that's why it never happened with those *other* girls. You're trying to please me too much. I love you for that.

I kept on talking as though I knew what I was talking about. Some atavistic wisdom I'd never heard from before, some benevolent, wise great-great-great-grandmother showed me how to be strong and firm even about things of which I had no knowledge. I could not let Larry's colors fade. I had to help him. You are the most sexy, desirable, lovely man in the world, and this will pass, I swear it, I told him, my heart in my mouth, knowing in my soul I would never have children. Honey, it will pass, I said, grinning. Let's get up and take a walk.

It passed. Larry, with gratitude, dates his present, awesome, often pesty virility back to that week.

Listen—no one is the world's champ at marriage, but I know this: We've got to give to each other the gift of unconditional love, of support, of acceptance. Love has no sure routes. You can murder the spirit, make the colors fade in many ways. This is the message I send my husband: There is so much we know about each other; I know your eyes by heart, I could kiss a thousand lips and know yours, I can cup my hands just so—and feel your face fit in them perfectly. So what if our bodies or our thoughts scare us sometimes? If I'm with you, you be with me, and nothing can get us.

When I asked him if I could write about this, Larry hesitated for a long time. "Try to be discreet," he finally sighed.

9

3

NO MULLET FISHING

When you're upset, let the other know—even
if you seem crazy.

⌣

I have to keep reminding myself that I'm not a murderer every time I lift a flailing flounder out of the water.

What can I do, Fish, my marriage demands this, I explain.

What can I do, Fish, we're all part of a giant food chain, I tell him. I'll lunch on you, but what squirmy killie was *your* lunch?

Doesn't help a bit. After I justify myself to the fine, fat flounder, I begin identifying with the still hooked and wriggling bait fish, still miraculously swimming post—flounder catch.

The fact is, I've never completely mastered this—it still bothers me. So, I make up my own rules to soften the killing ethic.

If, for example, we've baited the line with a brave, squirmy killie, and he doesn't attract a keeper fish in ten minutes *or* if we hook a fish and the killie's still alive and he still looks peppy (*it*—it still looks peppy), that killie's history: I carefully unhook him (*it*—unhook *it)* and send it gently on its merry way to tell God knows what horror stories to its sons and daughters.

Another rule is the No More Than I Can Freeze For The Bouillabaisse rule.

Another rule, of course, is the size rule: If the fish is undersize and especially if he's cute—say if he's yellow or blue—he's returned to his watery home.

Another rule is The Children rule: If there are any children on board who are likely to be traumatized by fish death, we throw the fish back.

It's a miracle we bring any fish home, Larry protests. Come *on!*

Steven Harber, Larry's fishing buddy, curses silently under his breath. Tell you who he'd like to send to a watery home.

———

Once I read a poem by Robert Penn Warren and, that night, woke in a cold sweat.

The Red Mullet

The fig flames inward on the bough, and I
Deep where the great mullet, red, lounges in
Black shadow of the shoal, have come. Where no light may

Come, he, the great one, like flame, burns, and I
Have met him, eye to eye, the lower jaw horn,
Outthrust, arched down at the corners, merciless as

Genghis, motionless and mogul, and the eye of
The mullet is round, bulging, ringed like a target
In gold, vision is armor, he sees and does not

Forgive. The mullet has looked me in the eye, and forgiven
Nothing. At night I fear suffocation, is there
Enough air in the world for us all, therefore I

Swim much, dive deep to develop my lung case, I am
Familiar with the agony of will in the deep place. Blood
Thickens as oxygen fails. Oh mullet, thy flame

Burns in the shadow of the black shoal.

Shivering from my dream, I climb out of bed in the night, go to find the poem, shake Larry awake, and read it to him.

" 'The mullet has looked me in the eye and forgiven nothing,' " I repeat loudly.

Patiently, seriously, he listens, forcing his eyes to stay open. Because he loves me, he will not trivialize what I feel. He knows this is no laughing matter.

We don't fish for mullet, he says when I'm all done. If you want another rule, you can make one: No Mullet Fishing, Ever.

Strangely, I'm comforted, and I can sleep.

4

A GOOD BOAT

_Tend the superstructure of the marriage. Don't
let it accumulate dry rot, never aim for its
humming heart, cherish its dignity._

~

If you want a boat, you need a good one. Not a fancy
number with a shower and separate cabins (although you
wouldn't hear me knocking that), but a boat that's crafted
with love and care, a boat whose powerful superstructure can
make up for navigational errors, a boat that nurtures as well
as pleasures. A good boat is more forgiving of human mis-
takes than a showy boat that's good only for taking Larry's
clients out for a spin in the harbor. It may be stretching the
Tao of fishing a bit, but there's a strong connection between
a good boat and a good marriage.

———

Whatever problems we have during our fishing day, a good
boat makes it easier to get on with the business of catching
a fish or getting home safely. We trust her. No ugly surprises
here. You don't have to worry whether the fittings will come
loose or the motor drop dead or the back end fall off if we
hit a log. For instance, when the winds are high and the water
spits and lashes at the cockpit, you have no choice but to pay
attention and face the fury. But at other times the sea fools

you and the waves rock you into a false security as they grow higher and lethal. If we're not paying enough attention, just drifting absentmindedly, a wave on the beam will wake us up but won't knock us over because the *Sherry J.* has a substantial keel underneath the water—the part that the clients can't see. She's a good boat with a strong superstructure that is protection against a blow on the beam.

A strong, loving feeling is also protection against a blow on the beam; nit-picking spouses drain loving feelings. Whatever problems we have with our work and our other relationships, we usually can get on with the business of dealing with them because we have no heartache from each other. We never have to feel gut-aggravated by something the other said or didn't say.

Larry and I tend our superstructure. We make very sure we don't allow dry rot to accumulate in the fittings or flail away at the essential framework.

In a marriage, this takes restraint. In our marriage, although we talk about everything, we don't let it all hang out. We don't go for the jugular.

When, for the fortieth time in a row, he's ordered too short a haircut and too long a cuff on his new suit trousers because his personal and sartorial habits haven't evolved since 1952, Keep your mouth shut, I say to myself, show your grit. So what if His Gorgeous doesn't show (I want it to show!) and he looks, well—alarmingly 1952 at a nineties party. *Keep your mouth shut.* Think about his sweetness.

Instead of nagging him about his GI Joe scalp, if I lightly run my hands over the nasty stubble and murmur in my best Marlene Dietrich voice, "Hmmmm—if it vas only a vee bit longer, it would drive me *crezy*"—then, for the next two or three haircuts, at least, he restrains his barber's savage fingers.

And when, for the fortieth time in a row, I drown him out at the party with my version of a story he's started to tell, he smiles tolerantly and grits his teeth with humor instead of saying, Do you *mind?* You're *interrupting.*

I know I've been rude to interrupt, and I'm so grateful he hasn't embarrassed me by calling attention to my steamroller technique, I won't do it *too* soon again.

———

In the end it comes to this: Each is responsible for the other's feelings. We express frustration, we give a voice to anger. But this is the cardinal rule: There is a hallowed point beyond which no temporary anger can be articulated. If we aim for the jugular, there is too much danger for both of us. Cruel words make us tongue-tied, cold-souled, make us want to hurt each othei.

So, we're careful; we never gain our strength by sapping the other's. We always try to think about protecting the dignity of "us" because if we chisel away, even at a good boat, we sink.

5

YOU HAVE TO HAVE

BEEN THERE

*Spend time together: hearing about catching
the shark isn't the same as feeling
shark's breath.*

The voice that comes out of my mouth when Larry suggests
shark fishing is like a winter coat: dark, draggy, and heavy.
I do not like shark fishing.

Once, I tell Larry, in the belly of a tiger shark, they
found a fur coat, a bottle of champagne, and a horse's head.

He ignores me.

Once, I tell him, I read in *Life* magazine that a thirty-
four-year-old woman named Shirley Ann Durdin left her four
children building sand castles on the beach and went off
to snorkel in six feet of water and was bitten in half by a
great white.

We'll leave at four, he says.

People *need* sharks, I tell him. I read that it's ecologically
unsound to kill them. Man is slaughtering sharks at a rate of
one hundred million a year. Scientists study them to find
anticancer agents, sharks keep the ocean healthy by preying

on sick and injured fish, shark corneas can be transplanted onto human eyes.

Sharks, I say sadly, are seriously threatened with extinction—it takes them fifteen years to reach sexual maturity, and most of them reproduce only once every other year, and then people like you go out to decimate the whole population. That's really immoral, you know, I say, warming to the task.

Take your knee boots, he says.

I play my last trump card.

I'll make love *all night* if we can stay home and go to a museum instead of shark fishing.

This slows down the plans, but only for a second.

Maybe we should leave earlier, he says.

———

I figured out that I can live our life sitting on the sidelines or I can be there for the ride. It doesn't take a rocket scientist to know that I would feel angry, resentful, watchful for his return on Saturday afternoons. I'm resourceful, Sisters, honest—there's much I can find to do or read or see, but when Larry's playing, when he's *available*, I want to play with him—even though it's not my game of choice. We both work hard. Like most couples, many of our marriage hours are spent apart. Forget this quality time; in child rearing and marriage it's quantity, hourly buildup, that counts.

That's why Larry often comes with me to writers' meetings or to interviews I have to conduct or speeches I have to give—even though his eyes glaze over and even though no one looks at him. But I know he's there, and we can touch in the taxi on the way home.

So if his hunger is for shark fishing, here I am shark fishing, yet again, with two of his macho fishing cronies. Golf, I think, probably could be worse.

————

I take myself out of the on-boat preparations and watch the diamond-studded water. We know there's a shark circling unseen, but close by: you can tell by the bait fish that are tossing frantically out of the heaving sea, chased by the shark. These tiny sacrifices are spinning off marbles of seawater, and they are wild things. On board there's a sickening overload of male bonding that's taking place—a lot of laughing and back slapping that has nothing to do with me. I stare out at the horizon. My world ends abruptly at the prow of the boat, and there a larger, more mysterious one begins.

When a shark is on, and the reel screams to tell us so, Larry and his cronies explode: tackle is flung away, the other lines are reeled up hurriedly so they won't tangle the shark line, men elbow me out of the way—fishing etiquette jumps overboard—Hey, there are *girls* on this boat, you know! I yell in an atavistic, prefeminist fury, but no one listens.

I stay out of the way when I'm not trying to prove something, and when I am, I usually hurt my back reeling in the fish. To tell the truth, it's not the heat of the battle but that time when the fish is finally landed in which I'm most interested—unlike the men, who are already rebaiting the hooks, on to the next challenge.

I'm drawn to the catch, the weird, primordially strange fish, hanging on the gin pole outside the boat. I stare at its alien self, a little embarrassed, and I silently apologize to it:

splendidly mad, brave fish—still fighting for its life. It's dangerous, but I run my finger along its raspy skin.

———

Something's happened here beyond the killing. By standing next to my husband in his moment of heart-stopping excitement, I have shared the essence of his adventure; I've actually felt the sensation of charged air in his chest. It wouldn't have been the same if I'd just heard the story about how they caught the shark. Being there with him, being *in* the story as he tells it to others, forges a bond more unbreakable than 250-pound wire fishing line.

6

RITUAL, SEA, AND

EARTH

Create love rituals. Make sure number one is:
Always pull socks on the other's cold feet.

Before you steam out to sea, you always have to do the same boring things. I'm impatient to start on the suntan and eat the cheese Danish and hear my favorite bell buoy's mournful warning and begin the *Kon-Tiki* fantasy that I'm all alone on this ocean (because, look, there's no other boat around). I also personally think it's prudent to be the first boat of the day to arrive at the fishing grounds so my aggressive self can hustle what I'm sure is the only waiting tuna right onto the hook. But noooo.

Larry has to perform the boat rituals.

They are incredibly tedious, and he does them over and over again, no matter if he did them just twenty-four hours ago. For instance, in the dawn's pink and before we turn on the engines, Larry must check the water levels, sniff the bilge for gas, open the windows, shmooze for five minutes with Ronnie, the bait master, sip a cup of coffee with the marina hangers-on, and sing "America the Beautiful" as he lets loose the lines that hold us to our earth moorings. Even I know that the boat would not move if one of these rituals were left out.

But why does he have to check the oil *every* time we leave the dock? You don't in a car, and besides, he checked it when we returned last week. And when we're exhausted and steaming into port, why does he have to stop at the gas dock to "top off" the tanks? And why does he have to test the radio, the Loran, the fish finder? They all worked last week. And coming into the harbor, why can't he take the shortcut, skip the buoy markers? Everyone else does it. But nooo, not Larry, he sticks to form. Rules and ritual. He says they contain, protect, and sanction. He says they're necessary.

Ritual attends our life off the boat as well.

1. *If one feels cold while watching television, the other gets up, finds the thick woolen socks, and pulls them on the cold one's feet. It is not enough just to get the socks.*

2. *If one takes a briefcase to work, the other writes a note and puts it in—no matter how many times you've written the same note.*

3. *If one goes away overnight, he/she leaves a note on the pillow.*

4. *If one has to work in the office on a Sunday, the other brings the newspaper and goes along for company, and is* quiet.

5. *Even if wildly busy, one stops a moment to telephone the other during the workday.*

6. *Hold each other soundlessly for one minute under these circumstances: when you come together again in the evening, when one feels nervous, and when the company leaves.*

7. *Even if watching a great movie on the VCR, one stops a moment to go hug the other, who is reading in the next room.*

8. *Spoon fits at night. If one turns over, so does the other.*

9. *Regular touching.*

10. *Best of all, the story-telling ritual: when one feels angst, the other makes up a glorious, happy-ending story starring the angst-ridden. It always starts with "Once upon a time" and usually comes true.*

7

N A M I N G

We become what we name each other.
Call me Rascal and watch how cute and rascally
I get. Call me Stubborn and watch.

We skim along the sea surface, and the day is so outrageously brilliant, it seems fake. Airy, ivory gulls colonize the sky. Clouds skitter by.

Sun blaze has lit the water like a photoflood, and the sparkly effect is almost blinding; to make the day even more glorious, crisp, cool breezes temper the sun's wattage.

It brings out the sublime in a person. Also, it brings out the boat jerks.

Boat jerks abound. Sometimes their boats are missile-shaped projectiles called "Cigarettes," and at a zillion miles an hour they hurtle past the Old-Man-and-the-Sea lobsterman, the early morning dreamers casting out ruminative sea lines, and reasonable folk like Larry and me. Hellish wakes fan out from their rocket tails: they tumble the old fisherman from his slatted rowboat seat, tangle the caster's pitch, and irritate the hell out of me. I mean, they *could* slow down a microsecond when they pass a quiet boat.

Sometimes boat jerks live on saner craft—but they're still jerks. Instead of giving way as sea rules prescribe, they rudely cut off tacking sailboats. They lie when you ask them over the boat radio if the blues are biting because they want all the blues for themselves. And worst of all, I've lately begun to notice, they give their boats jerky names.

I think that what you call a thing almost always has an effect on the thing named. Name a boat *Top Gun* and it's instantly reborn to surge violently, act hostile, aggressive, angry. Name a boat *Ride 'Em Cowboy* and a proud sea vessel becomes a rodeo act.

What you name a thing also gives *you* away. A guy who calls his boat *Sons and Lubbers* is a jerk with literary pretensions. A woman who names her boat *Instead Of* will never really be satisfied with the boat she bought instead of the mink, instead of the trip, instead of the house. A person who names a boat *Seas the Moment* or *Seaducer* is a cornball with whom I'd like no truck. And you'd want to steer clear of the person who owns *Night Stalker.*

It takes away a craft's dignity to call her *Uh-Oh* or *Water Toy* or *Drain Bamaged* or *Deep Throttle* or *The Codfather.* Such a craft will get even with you one day.

When a boat is named for a male owner, almost invariably it's a jerky name. I don't know why this is so, but spend a day in our busy harbor, see *Antnee* (clearly, Anthony's mother yelled out the window a lot for him to come home), *Ship of Jules,* and *Rubi-Yacht* (after an accountant named Rubinstein), and you'll know I'm right. And I have no words at all for the boat named *Murray* and her owner.

On the other hand, I'd like to meet the people who named their boat *Oxygen*—as in you have to have it to breathe freely. Or *Magic Carpet*—think what they expect of their lives afloat! Or *Goodness.* I want to spend the holidays with the people who know Goodness when they see her.

I want to give a medal to the sturdy Coast Guard cutter that picked up a raftful of exhausted Haitian refugees; fittingly, its name was *Confidence*.

Many families name their boats after themselves, as in *The Busy B's* or *The Salty C's*, but most use the name of a woman—a cherished wife, lover, mother, or daughter in their lives: for some reason, tradition says boats are female, as in *"She* went down at sea" or the *Queen Mary* as opposed to, say, the *King George*. It's nice to name a boat after a woman, even if it's uninspired. Our boat is named after me, and Larry would not hear of anything else, even though I came up with some splendid alternatives. Secretly I'm thrilled he would not be moved from *Sherry J.*

This business of name effect is powerful in marriages, too. Nice, funny, romantic names—and I don't mean just the names your parents gave you—are the currency of marriage, the coinage of happy families. Tender names, nicknames, sweet names, baby names, grab-ass names, poetic names, metaphor names, promissory names, make good connections. Bad names make sour connections.

———

Sticks and stones may break your bones, but names will never harm you? Wrong. Names are a million times sharper and more deadly than sticks and stones. Call a kid *stupid,* call him *irresponsible,* and he'll grow up stupid and irresponsible. Call a lover *wimp* and he'll wimp out. Even *insinuate* that a man is *bad in bed* or *clutzy*—and forget bed.

Don't be afraid to sound silly and call your mate *little,* and the *largest,* most aggressive, strongest, most fearless person will feel sheltered and adored.

Larry calls me Little. It sounds so embarrassing and maudlin. You have to be there. Little Sher is what he actually calls me. When he's not calling me *rascal* (in Paris it was *rascalette*, in Madrid *rascalita*, in Moscow *rascalnikov*).

The fact that I'm the least rascally person you ever met and, certainly, far from the littlest has nothing to do with it. I become rascally when he sees that in me.

———

I call him *friend*.

I call him *gorgeous*.

I call him *L.L.* There's no way I'll tell anyone why.

PART 2 TIDES

The Ebbs and Flows, the Ups and Downs

8

QUENELLES IN THE MACKEREL

*See the beauty in what he loves, even if it
looks, for a minute, like ground-up fish bait.*

Deep inside, what I really like best in the world is being in
our bedroom, just the two of us, eating Chinese food and
watching PBS. But then I read in the newspaper about this
fabulous party where Norman and Norris held sway or about
the Greek restaurant in Greenwich Village where Madonna
hangs out or about that interesting couple who stage James
Joyce readings on New Year's Eve with their fabulous, famous friends, and—I get nervous. Maybe we're missing
something. Maybe we should reach out. Open our marriage
to the bizarre, the brilliant, the original. I've always believed
it energizes a relationship when a couple is exposed to
inventive influences, original thinkers. So I've turned into a
sort of hunter and gatherer. I hunt for "interesting" people
who will expand our consciousnesses: I stage happenings in
my living room. I work hard to search out the colorful,
unfamiliar, intriguing.

Because I'm a journalist, this is not difficult. Last year I
covered Elizabeth Taylor's party, where Larry talked fishing

with Merv Griffin. For my story on dwarfs, Larry, at six one, towered over little people for weeks. Recently we had an Afghan Freedom Fighter sleeping in our spare room.

Larry usually smiles with amusement and some level of interest and goes along with my frenetic activity level on behalf of enriching our lives.

Every now and then he says, Cool it. Relax. Let's go fishing.

So, we do.

————

A bias against fisherpeople used to exist, dare I admit it, in my very own breast. Larry's fishing cronies were different from him—so anti–poetry reading, so anti-ERA, so anti–words of more than two syllables. Frequently and early in our marriage, I'd shoot antipiscatorial digs at my husband.

"We don't have much in common with these people," I used to say. "I know they're kind and they're marvelously colorful characters, but, well, they're really not part of our world. Look, I love you, but can't we just go to a movie instead of the annual boatyard picnic?"

I learned (it took some time) to give respect to that which brought happiness to my mate. I learned not to be judgmental of Larry's fishing pals and the salty, smelly milieu in which they all love to hang out and shoot the breeze and, God help me, talk Tackle.

At the marina where we keep the boat, there is a bait station, Ronnie's bait station. It is afloat in many men talking Tackle as well as in squid, worms, eels, chum (which is ground-up fish guts), killies, mackerel, lures, week-old herring—all the disgusting stuff that goes on the end of a hook. Sometimes, when I see Larry tossing this glop around, arms happily embedded up to the elbows, I secretly think, Never, never expect to touch me with those hands again. (But then, oh! those hands, washed.)

Ronnie Bauer, the proprietor of the bait shop, is a sun-grizzled, good-looking guy with twinkly blue eyes, an avuncular interest in my work, and a nice sense of humor. Once when I confided that I was ghostwriting a book for one of the great female tycoons in history, he asked, "She buy her bait here?"

Ronnie never ever leaves Freeport, Long Island, the small, oceanside town where the marina is located; he says he has everything he needs there, everything *anyone* would need.

So one day Ronnie says, Come over real early, first light—5:00 A.M.—before you go out fishing—and I'll show you around the harbor. Show me around? The harbor? Where I have to come, too often, anyway?

But Larry wants to go. So we get into a dilapidated rowboat with a muffled motor and the remains of an old lobster trap in its prow, and Ronnie quietly pilots us through the green velvet wetlands. The early morning is chilly, still, overcast, and, at first glance, quiet and empty of life. Every now and then the dark, glass-flat water is dimpled with the lazy rises of errant moss-bunker fish. I yawn loudly. Ronnie shushes me. If something wonderful isn't about to happen, why are three grownups sitting in a dirty rowboat at five in the morning without even a fishing line out in the water?

And then the show begins. Six long-legged, golden-shoed white herons appear, stalking the zillions of surface school fish. Each is magnificent and mesmerizing as he delicately, tentatively places each mile-long stick leg on the mossy ground cover as if he were tiptoeing in between hot coals. Ronnie hands me a pair of salt-encrusted binoculars and points: at first I see nothing, then a rare blue heron stalks in the midst of the tall sea grasses. Blue. Over there's a nest of fluffy, baby egrets—oh, they are adorable, yelling their lungs out for their mom. And just there, Ronnie points out a loving pair of green-and-black mallards looking for all the world like phony decoys. A flock of black Canada geese takes off with a *whoooosshh* five feet in front of me. The water's *alive*, and so is Ronnie, a veritable National Geographic guide, offering us a running commentary on the nonstop action in these narrow, tidal channels. He gently lifts a clump of kelly green moss, and underneath—voilà!—an uncooked bouillabaisse of clams, snails, mussels, and oysters all doing the Mollusk Thing. Who knows how many species of mosses, molds, lichen, weeds, herbs, grasses, and wild mushrooms grow in these lush marshlands? Ronnie does. Whom do I want to be with if my ship wrecks on the desert island? Ronnie.

Then—"Watch," he whispers, and he whistles an odd whistle. A huge, snowy-white, wide-winged heron appears from nowhere and flies directly to us. He perches on the oarlocks of the boat, and his proximity makes me gasp. Do herons get tangled in your hair? This one is a love slave to Ronnie, who feeds him a silver minnow from his pocket.

The wildest of creatures—and Ronnie has quieted and tamed him to come when called.

I can't get over this: I'd pay fifty dollars just to hear the man lecture at the New School, let alone get to see the show that's unfolding before us.

Wonderful, original experiences are all around us. It's all in the way you look at things, I guess, really look at them. Oh, God—not mackerel fishing, I said to Larry last week when mackerel season was upon us. I hate mackerel. Don't think of them as mackerel, he answered. Think of them as *quenelles de maquereau* served with a subtle *rémoulade* and some herbed cucumber spirals. This is because he brings fish to Madame Bonté, the elegant proprietor of the fantastic French bakery across the street, who lusts for fresh fish and rewards him with treasures like croissants and madeleines. So when I'm whimpering to get home already, we have *enough* mackerel, Larry's been known to say, Don't think of it as "just another mackerel"—think of it as *éclairs chocolat*, perhaps *une tarte poire.*

I have to learn to stop stage-managing our lives and pay more attention to real people and living ideas; try harder to see the quenelles in the mackerel. For starters, I've really come to love those guys who talk Tackle down at the marina.

Then I think I must learn to open our marriage to the fullness of ordinary days, dig deeper into old friends and family, and quiet the circus atmosphere. P. T. Barnum once put up a sign—THIS WAY TO THE EGRESS—and drew thousands of freak seekers who found themselves on their way out.

This Way to the Egret.

9

AUDIBLE STROKES

*Speak your love out loud. Saying it often—
saying it enough—makes it invincible.*

Larry wants me to love our boat, wants me to love it out loud, wants me to *say* good things about it with unqualified reverence.

I know what it means to him, so I tried. In the beginning, naturally, I qualified my reverence; since I come from a long line of qualifying matriarchs (It's great you're editor-in-chief; next year maybe you'll be president? You look lovely in that dress, darling—when you lose weight, you'll be really beautiful), this approach seemed the most truthful path.

"What a honey of a hull she has, how great the new flybridge seat looks, I much admire her underpinnings," I'd say, "but if only her paint weren't flaking, or her cabin were larger, or she had a real toilet with a door. Is that too much to ask for—a door?"

Didn't work. The stroking disappeared in the qualifications. Larry's face fell time and time again. But, if the truth be told, I felt foolish praising an imperfect boat with such glowing strokes. In my heart it was an okay, far-from-perfect boat: why shouldn't I tell the entire and absolute truth?

As the first months, then years, of our marriage passed, I reveled in the way Larry told me, every day of my life, how beautiful this or that part of me was and how he loved me. I knew how imperfect my nose was, or how unglamorous my too short, broken nails, but it was those parts that he *particularly* loved, he said.

Once, with great effort, I grew inch-long nails, painted them scarlet.

"Where are the little stubbies?" asked Larry. "Bring back those adorable stubbies."

Sure, it was silly. So what? I loved him for the saying of it.

And so I got into the habit of unqualified stroking, audible stroking. You have to say it right and say it out loud. Just saying it makes you feel cherishing and cherished.

———

So when I notice that Larry is self-consciously touching the little roll around his waist, I tell him what a darling roll it really is, how I love every inch. Somehow, saying this silly, absurd thing makes it true. I find I really do love best of all that part of him that's less than perfect. And when he's dreaming when he's supposed to be driving and he misses the turnoff that takes us to the expressway, and I start to complain, and he says in his own defense, "Sure—I *could* have done the popular thing, but I know how you hate the expected," then I laugh, and hug him, and tell him how funny he is and how insanely in love I am with his insane self.

My face sags with the weight of fifty years; Larry gently strokes my cheekbones and says with such cheekbones, I'll never look old—just check out Hepburn. Even though sanity tells me that Hepburn and I don't belong in the same breath, let alone beauty pageant, I still feel my face lift instantly. And when the children accuse me of being manipulative or pushy, Larry turns it around and tells me what a strong *force* I am, what a fierce protector of our family I am, not pushy at all. Look—I *know* I'm pushy (you always know when you're pushy), but when my husband turns it into a virtue, I am forever grateful to him for sticking up for me. Also, I'll stick up for him the next time he blunders down the wrong road and everyone else in the car yells.

So we don't qualify our stroking because we have reverence for the—forgive the expression—love boat. When we're hopelessly lost and he just won't ask directions (male inbred trait), I never—well, hardly ever—tell him he's stubborn, foolish, and exasperating. I try to grin and bear it because he grins and bears my weaknesses without ever chipping away at my heart with scissor words.

———

This sounds like we're saints. Wrong. We are not saints. But we've learned that when one verbally strokes, speaks her love with clear, unqualified words, then the other is heavily induced to respond in kind.

Audible strokes, like the even claps of a dinghy's oars as they connect with, then caress, the water.

10

COMMUNITY OF TWO

Be an island. Sting if the world moves
in too close.

Sometimes I just like to hang dopily over the side of the boat, watching the sea creatures slide by. The ones I find most compelling are the jellyfish—the ones that look like accidents, simple blobs in the water. Secretly I treat them as metaphors: they help me find my ground, help me focus my willy-nilly thoughts. In a way that I don't quite understand, this alien sea life is familiar. It often reminds me of me—and of my marriage.

A jellyfish is wafting by this minute, even as I write in my journal. It's a round, translucently milky creature that floats the surface as we cruise. It undulates around and under the boat with seductive mystery, coming very close—then shifting off. It hypnotizes me.

People think of the jellyfish as a weak, insipid thing, but I know it is a small, deceptively sturdy island, complete in itself. I stare at it, tempted to reach over and touch. But I don't. It has an awful sting. I can watch it, circle it, even play with it a bit by letting it swim over and around a net handle I hold in the water: what I can't do is invade its center by prodding or testing. If I try, it swims quickly away. Or stings.

This may sound unfriendly, but on some level I think of that free-floating island jellyfish as the marriage we've created over long years. Larry and I connect with the world on our terms, but we've learned not to be its landlady. We don't invite friends to stay with us for long periods of time, and even the beloved out-of-town relatives know their days in the spare room are numbered. Don't even *think* about calling us after nine P.M. We're letting the day go, we're busy reconnecting.

Our community is one of two. We've heard about the goodness that happens when the nuclear family gives way to the extended family—aunts, uncles, grandparents, and pals all rallying around, all having an equal vote.

We love the grown kids, but thanks, we'll still take just the two of us, bobbing along, playing with others, but in the end just we two.

Because, ultimately, our island is inviolable. I mean by anyone. No loyalty, not to parents, children, or friends, is stronger than our unit. We've come to be exquisitely careful not to carelessly prod our marriage or test it unmercifully. Some of us—read, Larry—are more careful than others; however, we both warn each other when danger looks appealing.

———

Once, in the pre-AIDS experimental seventies, danger looked appealing. I'd met an extraordinary woman, a physician, beautiful, strong, an original thinker. Whenever I left her, I was invigorated and challenged. She was a free spirit, and she made me feel bright and funny. The best part was that her marriage sounded very like mine—wonderful. Her eyes shone when she spoke of her husband. "We'll have to all go out for a drink," she said, "one day."

We did. Her husband was a classical Shakespearean actor, straight from Central Casting. The four of us hit it off splendidly, and we spent several months sopping up the good of each other, cooking for each other, delighting in our new friendship. Also, we laughed a lot.

And then the other shoe hit. This wonderful couple, with the most infinite tact, ever so gently suggested we stretch our friendship to include sex—four ways. It would, they said, only lend richness to each already wonderful marriage. It would expand our experience. It would not be an extramarital experience since we'd all be involved, all consenting. It would be lovely, they said.

I was shocked—but inexplicably aroused. I knew, deep inside, that I could never go beyond fantasy, but something made me want to test Larry to be *sure* he wasn't tempted, to be sure he couldn't be talked into it. What would I do if he failed the test? I didn't know.

Later, at home, I thought about it, out loud, with my husband.

Larry never broke stride.

"Are you crazy?" he asked me. "*Titanic* danger!"

And then, I'll never forget what he said next.

"We will *never* violate this safe place, this sanctuary," he said.

Gradually we lost touch with our entrancing friends.

———

I've learned to guard against putting our relationship into profound or even shallow jeopardy. We're not exactly inhospitable jellyfish; friends and family can visit, but no one can live in our interior space. No one, even an entrancing someone, can hitch on to it.

Don't ever say to me, "Don't tell Larry," because, depend on it, I will. I'll be your pal, I'll do anything for you if you are my real family or my extended family of friends, but with my own heart, I trust only him. He's my one true mate.

We share the same agenda.

Jellyfishlike, we make an island. Not that our island is a paean to isolation. All islands are connected to water, other islands, sky, swimming creatures. I think that our separateness is not a disconnect from the world but a way to better understand relatedness.

Still, no one is allowed to annex our island. No one is allowed to prod it. We will back off. We will sting.

11

PATIENCE

*Hold your horses, bide your time, cool your
heels: eventually, the bait looks interesting
to the fish.*

~

We both bait up, cast out, and hang around companionably,
waiting for the first bite.

He can sit there for hours, waiting.

I wait a few minutes, then I jiggle my line around a lot and
reel it up three times in the next ten minutes to make sure
there's still bait on the line. Then I change the bait because
the little, furious killie has put in his time and needs to be set
free. Then I put my rod in the rod holder and go to lie down
in the deckhouse to listen to some jazz on my Walkman.
Then I eat my midmorning snack, then I eat part of Larry's.
Then I fiddle with the ship-to-shore radio to listen to the
Coast Guard getting SOSs. Then I ask the Coast Guard for
a radio check to make sure they can hear me if I need to give
an SOS. Then I take my rod from the rod holder and change
the bait again. Then I tell Larry about the flyer I've seen this
morning on the grimy wall of the Hudson Point Fishing
Station:

WANTED: Good woman with boat and motor. OBJECT:
matrimony. Please send picture of boat.

Then I take a picture of Larry laughing. Then I tell him it's not funny, most fishermen are *like* that. Then I check my bait again. Larry is still waiting.

How can he do it?

Then he catches a thirty-pound striped bass.

Just lucky, I guess. Damn.

But the lesson carries. Whenever I don't have anything better to do, I consciously work on being patient. In a very real way, and even if it's counter to my nature, my growing ability to wait for my pleasures has served our marriage well.

———

Marriage is about many things: I've often thought that the truest essence of a great marriage is each seeing the other as unfailingly interesting. Also, I can't help feeling instant warmth for someone who likes me, so when Larry never seems to tire of my wit (such as it is) or touch, it's very seductive. And I do that for him, also. I daily massage his ego with my very real interest, and he knows that I sincerely believe every woman in the world would like to get her hands on those fetching knees.

I also believe that *wanting to come home* is key to a good marriage. You only want to come home if there's peace when you arrive. The rare and fine part of our lives is the calm in our house. When you get there, it's easy, it's nice, you love it, you put your answering machine on, no one can get to you. You feel cherished and safe. No one is waiting in the wings to demand "How *could* you have done that—how could you be so dumb?" When all around you others are unloading on your head and you can go home and there's no judging, no criticism, no impatient sighs—just a warm holding of each other, some laughs, companionable silence till you read something you need to share with the other, and a knowledge that in just a few hours you'll probably be in bed together—well, that's something.

Marriage is about gentle ribbing but never cutting sarcasm. If he has a habit of Announcing everywhere he goes (I'm going to the basement. Now I'm going to the kitchen), as the ex-husband of my friend used to do, you *don't* spit out, "Have a good trip. Be sure to write."

Marriage is about defending your husband in public even when you waver in private. The day I told a racing sailboater who complained about the noise of power boats to just "tack off," my husband bellowed in admiration of me, "God, you were magnificent!"

But of all these important things to know about marriage, sometimes I think that patience is the most important of all; at least for me it is, and maybe that's because it was so hard to develop.

———

In the mornings we swim at the local Y. I hate it like poison. I hate every form of exercise. I don't *care* if my upper arms droop, I don't *care* if I'm a teeny bit breathless after a brisk walk to Bloomingdale's, I think they'll find out that jogging, in particular, is a secret, swift killer. The only thing good about swimming is that you do it lying down. I certainly hate the way the icy water grabs at my heart at eight A.M. It's abnormal, against all rules of nature to be in icy water at eight A.M. I hate the pool terrorist who, when passing in the narrow lane, would just as soon kick you in the groin as not. I hate the smell of the chlorine and what it does to my already seasoned skin. I hate the boredom of back and forth, back and forth. But even though I wake raging against the barbaric practice, every morning Larry drags me out to do my thirty-six laps. It's the only exercise I get, he says, and I owe it to us to do it. Grumbling mightily, I jump in that accursed pool.

To be scrupulously honest, no one—not even Larry—can make me do anything I hate doing. So why do I really swim?

For the breakfast afterward. During all thirty-six laps, I practice calm endurance as I ponder, Should I have the bagel or the Danish, the fruit salad or the cranberry muffin? Should we go to the new luncheonette on 92nd Street or back to Leo's on 86th Street? The laps drop away. Breakfast out is the ritual we share after the hated swim, a last time together till we meet again in the evening. This measly half hour brings such peace, such a sense of "all's right in the world," it sets me up for the whole day. We share our morning terrorist story, locker-room gossip, the newspaper headlines, and the plans for the evening movie. The breakfast is important to us.

If I want that nice breakfast, I have to suffer the boring swim. So I swim for my breakfast.

"It takes patience to appreciate domestic bliss; volatile spirits prefer unhappiness," wrote Santayana.

So I wait nicely for Larry to dine leisurely when I want

to *eat* and get to the movie; I calmly bide my time during the despicable boxing match; I cool my heels when he tells an interminable story; I hold my horses when he's reading the section of the newspaper I crave. I have the patience of a saint.

Sometimes.

12

TUNA ODYSSEY: THE
GREAT GIVE-BACK

Give some, get some: we take and give back
through all our days.

~~~

We'd been married nineteen years before Larry dared suggest we cruise for a month on the boat. *Live* on the boat for a *month!* Oh, no.

We had, by now, a twenty-eight-foot sportfisherman with a real toilet: still, twenty-eight feet ain't a heck of a lot of space in which to wander for twenty-eight days. But Larry had been a stoic, even an enthusiastic stoic, on God knows how many European and antiquing trips I'd dragged him on. This was the great give-back.

If you've crossed the Sahara by camel, if you've run the Iditarod dog race between Nome and Anchorage, if you've been lost in the steaming mountains of the Peloponnese, you're game. But not so game as you would be to live, to *sleep*, on a tiny boat in unfamiliar waters for a whole month with a mild attorney-husband turned mad fisherman.

For months he planned the trip. Wills were put off, trials postponed, and divorces abandoned in disgust because the lawyer was poring over his marine charts, figuring out courses and tide tables. For me it would be a test of endurance and a paean to togetherness. For him it was nothing much: just his life's dream.

We packed a minimum of clothes; secretly I thought I was adorable in my yellow foul-weather gear. Adorable my foot. I lived in it and blessed its water-repellent self during the two-day nor'easter.

Finally the course was plotted. We'd head east up Long Island Sound from our home port all the way to Point Judith, through Buzzard's Bay, the Cape Cod Canal, and then north to Gloucester. We'd pass points of land and towns with names like Noank, Beavertail Point, Cuttyhunk, Old Cock, Sippican Neck, Strawberry Point, and finally, outside of Gloucester Harbor, the fabled reef of Norman's Woe, where on a wintry sea the schooner *Hesperus* was wrecked.

I already knew one thing about the ocean that I dreaded: sometimes in our regular, little, local fishing forays, a sudden squall would hit. I learned to watch Larry's face for signs of imminent disaster as he kept the bow headed into the wind. I hated the sting of sudden driving rain and the heavy threat of lethal lightning.

"Rain is nothing," Larry would say. "It's the wind you have to watch out for. And worse, the fog."

Fog, fog—who could be afraid of romantic fog?

———

The first day out was a cliché of silver sky and amethyst sea. I lay on the deck while the sun baked deep: we were *years* away from SPF codes. I was getting a ton of give-back credit. Isn't that what marriage is all about—give and take? Hey, between you and me, this wasn't half-bad.

And then the wind hit. The waves weren't six feet high all at once. They grew gradually from a gentle hammering at the stern to a wind-propelled cataclysm of hellish energy. I clung to the flybridge, praying for anything else but punishing buffeting. Apparently my prayers were heard.

Because the wind died down and the fog came. So what, fog. Holding my hand in front of my face, I could not make out my fingers. Nor the huge apparition of a freighter that loomed out of the wet wool not thirty feet in front of us, blowing an angry whistle.

———

We got through it. That first evening we moored at Saugatuck, Connecticut, a lovely, sheltered harbor. We had the Sunday *Times* on board, Hershey bars, and a tape deck. The remnants of the fog enveloped us in a warm, sweet cocoon. We were totally alone. I was glad I didn't insist on turning back after the storm (it occurred to me). A gentle boat rocked us to sleep.

It is 4:30 A.M. We start while the horizon is clear and the weather holds. The sea's our own, endless and starlit at first, then rippled with a pale dawn light.

When—*what is this??* Something black, something oily, massive, and soundless begins emerging from the water fifty yards from our beam. I am terrified. It's all over for us. Larry bellows with excitement, "God damn——it's a submarine!"

It is. Do I have to worry about whether it's an enemy submarine? Larry says not to be my mother's daughter.

But this thing is *wild*. It slides unctuously through the water with staggering power. I'm hypnotized by the unrelieved silence of its operation. It is like some prehistoric creature. Then, as mutely as it appeared, the two-hundred-

foot monster disappears. A couple of bubbles, a soft hiss—
and it's gone.

Where? *Under* us? Larry says to forget about it.
Oh, sure.

———

We dock at Gloucester, and the next morning is set for the
Great Tuna Hunt. The sea is an immense lily pond, pregnant
with swells, each, I hope, a potential tuna birth. We catch a
tuna, maybe we can go home. Randy, the mate we've hired
for a hundred bucks, speaks with a strong, southern drawl.

"Good fishing today, Randy?"

"Fahnest kahnd. . . ."

The boat surges forward. Randy and Larry chum endlessly, throwing out huge chunks of chopped-up, stinky
mackerel, whiting, and "herrin' "—some of which gets on
me. After four hours we are lulled by the feeling of failure.
Then, "Right ahead—no—*there!*" Randy motions directly
ahead with his chin. He stares intently. I see nothing. More
sea. More swellings.

"There—now, look!" Now Larry points, and by God, I
see an infinitely graceful blue-back break the water just ahead
of the bow. Sliding silently in the water then, three huge,
shadowy shapes, slowly feathering deeper into the sea, until
I can no longer make them out. Good Lord—what are we to
do with creatures like this? *Catch* them? It would be like
catching the wind, I think, or catching a spirit. I am identifying with the fish again, I know it. Keep your mouth shut,
Sherry. Don't ruin it for him.

Suddenly we are surrounded by a horde of noisy, com-
peting sportfishing boats. The tuna keep their distance. Who
wouldn't?

"It was the pointing that did it," Randy says glumly. "Never point when you sight a fish. A fisherman can see a point thirty mahles away."

Next day—same scene, same characters. We go twenty miles farther offshore: perhaps the tuna live there.

Not twenty minutes after the chumming begins, one of the rods in the rod holders suddenly dips down and line begins screaming off the reel at an alarming rate. I stand looking at it, mesmerized, when a violent shove from my once gentle husband propels me out of the way. He hurls himself onto the fighting chair and begins to pump the now searingly hot reel, and then the rhythm begins, pump and reel, pump and reel, pump . . .

"Water!" yells Randy, and when I hand him a bucketful, he pours it over Larry and the reel. This, to me, is an antediluvian ritual. It is to be repeated many times. Finally the fish heads down under the boat somewhere while Larry frantically reels in loose line.

I remember getting very nervous at this point. My husband was panting, perspiring, and white of face. He was making groaning sounds. He had been fighting a monstrous, mindless creature for almost an hour. He was forty-six years old at the time and looked far from well. Everything that was my mother's child shrieked out at me: Cut the line. End this folly. Save your husband from a certain heart attack.

I didn't. Thirty thousand wife credits.

For a minute the fish comes into view, and it is glistening sterling and navy—a giant bluefin tuna with immense power. It must weigh over three hundred pounds. Suddenly it dives down out of sight. The rod is bent almost double. Larry and Randy are beside themselves with naked desire. With one clean, savage yank—the tuna breaks free.

Strangely enough, Larry's not devastated. It was the anticipation and the struggle that meant the most—and my being there, he tells me later. There's already talk of next year. The days flow by, enhanced by dozens of fluke feeding frenzies, decks bloodied by fish innards, one explosive marlin that somersaulted and tail-walked magnificently on the water surface. And quiet hours, quiet night talks.

On the way home, together, in the middle of an ocean, we fix a complicated and very broken engine, we who don't know how to fix a broken vacuum cleaner at home. We hug each other with new respect.

And then it was over. A month gone.

———

Once I took a cruise when I was single, on an elegant ocean liner. It was a pretty thing to do, but there was no melodrama of navigating through a blue fog, no scary submarine, no dropping of the anchor in a sweet and private ocean and seeing a perfect golden fish leap four feet out of the water in some kind of fishy exultation.

This is the real point of this tale. If you want a good marriage, you have to let him do what he needs to do even when it entails boredom or, worse, risk, terror, and stupidity. You don't have to love it, but you do have to get to understand it. And to some extent, God help me, share it.

On our tuna odyssey there was damp and mold in our pajamas and too many lumps on a convertible couch and too many hero sandwiches. But there was also the sharing of my husband's great love, the give-back for all his generosity when he shared my loves with me.

We take and give back through all our days.

13

FIDELITY

*The tides are constant, and you better
be, too; it's monogamy, honey,
or I'm out of here.*

〜

The tides are enduring, faithful, and constant. They will roll on and on, will not fail you, will not fool you, will not fall for a pretty blonde. The tides are not fickle.

People are. I've been married over thirty years, and occasionally I still have the dream. He comes to me in this dream, his beloved face in agony for what he has to say.

"There's this *p-person*," he stammers. "I could never imagine that I would be attracted to anyone else. I love you. I don't know what happened."

But *I* know what happened. He slept with a beautiful woman, that's what happened, he took a turn with Someone Else. In the dream, my heart shatters. Well, there's only one reasonable thing to do. I go get a gun.

Then I wake up. My chest hurts terribly in the place where my heart was, and it will for another hour.

Larry knows exactly what I've dreamed when he senses me frozen on my side of the bed. "Damn it—*again?*" he says. "It's a dream, honey. No turns. I didn't do it. I *wouldn't*."

I look at him suspiciously. He holds me hard.

I push him away.

The dream seems so real and I feel so violated that it's hard to let it go.

———

This is the question: If it wasn't a dream, would I still shoot him? Yes. Well—put it this way: even if sober thoughts about jail changed my mind about the gun, I'd definitely still leave him—even if he swore he'd never do it again, even if God promised it would be "only that one time." I'm out of here—no discussion.

Maybe more adventuresome couples find mutual joy in having affairs, maybe some women and some men can happily cheat on their mates, but in my heart of hearts I don't believe it. *No playing around, ever* is our rule—an enormously comforting one. It's the only possible way to have a great marriage: if you disagree, I'm right and you're wrong. How can you be profoundly intimate with someone who may be being profoundly intimate with someone else? Not possible.

I know all the arguments against leaving Larry if he should slip, even once:

1. *I'm childish, unforgiving, and unrealistic, and the kids would be devastated.*
2. *I'd be cutting off my nose to spite my face, this is the real world—grow up.*
3. *I need him for my legal problems—if I should ever have any.*
4. *He makes more money than I do.*
5. *I'd have to go places alone, sit in the back of my friends' cars.*
6. *It's insane to throw away all our shining history for just one mistake.*
7. *Everyone's entitled to one mistake.*

No, he isn't. I'm gone.

There are those who say that I'd be indulging in an act of self-sacrifice if I left him over a one-shot roll in the hay, someone else's hay. I see it as an act of control over my own life. I could fake forgiveness, I could rationalize onetime errors, but nothing in my nature says that I could ever live happily with anyone who betrayed me—even once.

"You want monogamy? Marry a swan," said a character in a movie I detested. I guess many people feel that way. In recent surveys, a staggering 70 percent of all men under forty said they could see themselves getting involved in an affair. Experts project that one in two women will have an extramarital experience—such is the appeal of strangers in the night. Keep your strangers in the night; I choose familiarity.

Some of the light will go from their marriages. It has to. I may be rowing against the tide, but on I go: an open marriage is a contradiction in terms. Marriages are closed.

Flashback: My marriage is twelve years old, and one morning I turn a corner and there he is—the poet I loved at college. We laugh in delight at the unexpected meeting and go for coffee. He recites for me the anguished poem he wrote on the night he heard I was going to marry Larry. Bells are going off in my head and my heart. This is *fun.* It's dangerous. I can't believe how excited I feel: my whole body is electrified by possibilities. How far should I take it, how far *can* I take it?

Not far, I suddenly know with absolute certainty. I could probably get away with it, but the risk that it would inalterably change our relationship is too profound. For me, forget forgiveness, nothing would ever again be the same. Imagine your *person* in the arms and bed of another. Tell me your own heart doesn't go belly up like a dead fish, tell me you'll forget the image one day. Sure you will.

I say good-bye to the poet.

———

I tell Larry to tattoo on his wrist the following lines from Matthew Arnold's "Dover Beach":
"Ah, love, let us be true / To one another!"

Make that both wrists.

———

Maybe a younger generation than mine is more open-minded. I ask my daughter if she thinks she'd be understanding if her young husband were unfaithful just one time.

"Death by hanging," says Jennifer.

The tides are constant, and you better be, too, or else, as a Guatemalan friend once said, "forget it about it."

14

BLUE WATER

Dependency *is not a dirty word.*
Risking reliance on another can
be the way to self-growth.

Where I live, the deeper the water, the bluer it gets—and you have to go many miles out to sea to find that unclouded cobalt blue color.

Much closer to home, the water is shallower—and muddier and darker. Blue doesn't enter the picture.

The part of me that fears danger just loves those muddy, murky shallows where the fishing is limited but the shoreline is close.

Larry is drawn to the blue water. Depend on me, he used to say when we first began to date. We'll go deeper, farther out, where the possibilities are endless: we could catch *anything* out there! You'll love it. Depend on me.

Depend on him? Not likely, I thought then.

Before I was married, I swam in the shallows. I cared deeply about being totally independent; for me, that meant rarely risking the blue water: it was the unknown. Too scary alone. But, so what: I'd do the things I could carry off myself.

When I was a teenager, although my parents were

always there for me, I felt uncomfortable about leaning on them, and I consciously worked on separating. A few years later, as young women just predating *The Feminine Mystique*, my friends and I got very good at playing games with men; pretend dependency, we told each other, but be, at all costs, totally self-reliant. Be whole, we thought, and we won't have to worry about being sapped by another.

But there were always problems. The being whole part sounded good, but still things never felt exactly right. First of all, although I'd always been for self-development, it was *hard* to develop a self in isolation. Also, I never really thought all that much of the separating theory. It always seemed to be so, well—*male*. Boys are taught early on to disengage in the name of growth: any nine-year-old male who still feels connected to his mom is suspect. Well, this kind of separation seemed self-denying to me because I knew that, like most women, connection—not separation—was what I was good at.

So, even if "self-sufficient" was my personal code word, I couldn't help but notice that my *self* never quite sufficed. Trying to think of my *self* as a strong but disconnected element only made me crazy. It gave me night willies. It felt as if there was too much I had to do alone, too much to figure out. I needed feedback, I needed my thoughts jogged by outside forces, someone else listening, someone else talking, even someone else disagreeing. Alone, it was night willies. I was no good disconnected.

I saw that many of my friends fell in love, sometimes married, and still always kept a part of themselves in permanent disconnect. After all, we were taught that self-protection meant avoiding dependence. Being whole meant holding back.

————

Ironically, my own sense of what was possible for me in this world developed only after I learned to make the deepest attachment to Larry. To depend on him. To venture out to the blue water. Because he knew how to get back, I began to feel sure I could do it myself. I became a strong woman precisely because I made a conscious decision to relinquish control, to follow his lead in some—not all—things. It was when I started thinking of *my* self in relation to *his* self, me feeling his needs, he thinking my thoughts—*then* I could say good-bye night willies, hello smarts, strength, and stretch. I used to be embarrassed to admit it, but now I think I've arrived at a profound truth. Sure you can make it alone, sure you can remain totally independent in marriage; it's better when you risk a connected dependency.

It's the connections that engage, enliven. When we empower another, we make two dazzling selves from two shrimpy ones.

So, concentrating on our relationship empowers Larry and me, makes us more than our two selves. We interact, we depend on, we trust, fail, and grow together: each self grows stronger. We get irritated with each other: patience, counsels the one who's *least* irritated. We sense weakness in the other or hear something that scares us, we swallow hard and embrace the other's weakness or need.

You want to spend our retirement money on *radar? Are you crazy??* Oh, okay, let's talk about it.

You want to go live in England for a year? How can we *do* that? Well, let's see. . . .

Weakness loses its capacity to wound, the stuff that scares is bearable because now, having embraced each other with humor and love, it's *our* weakness, not just his, it's our fear, not just mine.

———

But people have to *learn* to connect; have to learn *not* to sacrifice self or autonomy, but to make self more powerful through a true joining: that knowledge doesn't come automatically with the ring.

We've learned to make time to tell each other secrets. It was very hard and it took several years of marriage for Larry to tell me that he was sexually abused by an older boy when he was nine; once having told the secret shame, he freed himself of it and gave permission to himself and to me to talk about it openly.

It's a funny thing about secrets: telling a painful one to someone usually makes the other person want to tell one right back. So it wasn't as difficult as I thought to confide in my husband that secretly I felt like an imposter-writer, no real talent—and, lately, an imposter-mother who's failed miserably. But having told my worst fears, I'm able to deal with them.

We've learned not to trivialize the other's worries. Instead of brushing off my sure knowledge that I have skin, breast, lung, and brain cancer, Larry comes with me to the doctor to rule out the worries, neurotic or not.

We've learned to be loyal beyond description—*never* tell on the other. Friends are nice and children are swell, but it's you, Babe, *you.*

There is an ancient superstition of the sea that says, If you are very patient, inevitably one wave will come along that is greater than any that came before, and that will be a marvelous thing to see. It is called The Ninth Wave, and it's so potent because it's the powerful connection, the synergy of sea, wind, and tide—come together at one divine moment. An utterly independent tide, an utterly independent wind, an utterly independent sea could not a Ninth Wave make.

My parents are not connected. They have a difficult marriage. Individually each is interesting, loving, clever: together they are search and destroy—locate the weakness of the other, niggle it, jiggle it, get to the nerve, then drill. Instead of connecting, they separate. Instead of empowering, they complain. During my growing-up years, the family spoke with one dominant voice—usually my mother's—and one veto—my father's. Negotiation was what Presidents did. Each demanded sacrifices of the other. She would never learn that you could invest a husband with the strengths he doesn't own; he would never understand that stroking a wife empowered her; they never, ever in sixty years got it: connections don't drain—they replenish. Synergy wasn't a big concept Chez Suib, where blood was thought to be thicker than water, thicker certainly than a bond between two strangers who happened to marry each other.

Somehow, despite their own disconnect notice, they both managed to give me the best of themselves. My mother's fierce, protective instinct made me always feel safe. My father's love of language and stories gave me books. From my mother I learned I was important and special, and even though her dreams for me never can be completely satisfied, she let me know I had power to *become*. From my dad I learned I could be different and survive. But none of this did they give each other: their lesson about marriage was that it is the pits.

Thank God, despite what the Freudians say, I didn't have to marry my father, didn't have to search for my mother, I'm here as living proof that marital history doesn't have to repeat itself.

With my husband I can venture to blue water and return to safe harbor no matter how far out we go. I'm not sure, but I think that on my own, unlinked, overdefended, I'd still be swimming in the shallows.

15

CREATING INTIMACY

*True intimacy requires a dollop of mystery and
a tad of Victorian modesty.*

Sociologists speculate that the alarming decline in marriage
rates is likely caused by economic hard times, but I know
better: People are not getting married so much because they
fear and misunderstand intimacy. They think that profound
intimacy saps individuality. They want their own space, they
say. They don't want to be joined at the hip.

We're not joined at the hip, but we sure put in serious
time together. Friends ask how we can stand the closeness of
living on the boat for two vacation weeks of enforced intimacy, twenty-four hours a day. Stand it? Such closeness
enriches our marriage, gives it *moxie.* I don't mean to say we
don't have lives apart from each other, happy, productive
lives. Of course we have challenges, colleagues, and experiences that we enjoy separately in a tantalizing, vast world.
But once home, we are together—and we know how to *be*
together precisely because we spend long periods of time
invested only in each other. Two hundred hours alone on a
small boat in a wide ocean gives us practice for land.

Intimacy, for us, is sharing, not annihilating, the other's
uniqueness, the other's essence. The philosopher Gabriel

Marcel described it this way: "Even if I cannot see you, if I cannot touch you, I feel that you are with me." Exactly.

Here is the way we engender intimacy in our lives:

- If we are home together, we almost always stay in the same room—even when we are doing other things. We learned the worth of that on the boat, where there is no choice.

———

- We invariably wake at the same hour, leaving a little time for morning horseplay, and then always breakfast together. In the corner luncheonette, if I can help it. When pressed, I make smashing pancakes.

———

- If he is to leave at three in the morning for a shark tournament to which I can't go, I would be wild with anxiety if he didn't wake me for the good-bye kiss—*even though I know I'll never get back to sleep.* Then I read in the dark, quiet night for an hour or so, the kiss alive on my mouth.

———

- We don't vacation even with our most beloved friends. How can we recharge our intimacy with others around?

———

- We respect each other. I honor Larry by being careful about my appearance: I wear clothes and scents we both like. When he comes home, I'm the last word in cute. He does the same for me. I don't think this is a superficial concern. I'm a strong feminist, and so is he, and because of that we heed each other's sensibilities. We respect each other in our tones of voice and in what we say: we try not to be shrill, wheedling, judgmental.

———

- Sometimes we flirt, play games, make bargains with each other, just as we did when we were courting.

  ———

- Here's a big one. We revel in privacy. Intimacy doesn't mean lack of privacy. The capacity to be alone is vital in a good marriage; how else does one nourish inner resources, imagination? I cherish times of solitude, a return to my deepest self: I cherish it sometimes on a beach, sometimes at a museum, sometimes in my room, sometimes on a busy city street, and always in the bathroom.

  I have friends who use the bathroom together—she on the john while he shaves. It's perfectly *natural*, they tell me, and why am I so inhibited?

  I'd die. It seems to me that the dearest familiarity can be shattered by a certain kind of coarseness, a lack of modesty. True intimacy requires a dollop of mystery.

PART 3
CROSSCURRENTS

Conflicts: Moving Against the Flow

16

LANDMARKS

Lying, even a little, puts you in treacherous
water; getting your bearings in marriage
requires honesty in the small things.

Larry has lots of jobs to do at sea. He has to figure out whether the boat is secure, the tail rope is ready, the gaff is handy; he has to know the kind of bait to use, the kind of weather we'll have, the water depth, and where the tuna are holding their annual convention. I have only one job: to worry. Before we start and as we steam forward, I'm already figuring out how to get back. What happens if Larry is clonked on the head and it's my responsibility to navigate us safely to the Columbia Presbyterian Hospital emergency room? It's not as if I can hail a cab in two hundred feet of water. Even if I knew that north was the direction to home, I'd have no idea which way north was. Sure, we have a compass, but what if the compass got broken? What then? I ask you. What then?

You've got to get your bearings.

Getting your bearings means finding out where you are by recognizing landmarks. Sometimes, far out at sea, no landmarks are visible, but seamarks—the depth of the water and the shape of the sea bottom—can also help you gain your bearings—and get you to the emergency room.

It's not easy because the mirrored surface of the sea blinds me to the seamarks—the shape of the sea floor, not to mention the teeming life that exists underneath. A car operates on a flat plane in only two dimensions. A boat demands that you understand two more: what's under the water (the rocks and reefs and wrecks that are invisible but perilously real) and what's above it (those winds from balmy to tornado force).

So Larry has taught me various ways to read the signposts of the sea by the temperature of the water, the instruments that read the sea bottom, the various clues that reveal what I can't hope to see. I get my bearings to home even before I bait (okay, before he baits) my fishing line.

————

The way I see it, you've got to get your bearings in marriage. In order to find your way, you've got to settle on the marks that give you a direction to take. If you can learn to read what is hidden at sea—the water depth or the shape of a certain stretch of ocean floor—you can learn to read the not-so-visible signs in a relationship that give you your bearings, your sense of safety.

————

This is the hard part: Perfect trust is such a signpost. Sorry, but that's the way it is. If you lie about how much money you made on a certain deal or why you were late—such small things—it's still a lie, and it can wreck perfect trust. If your significant other should present you with just one little lie, it blurs the trust landmark from which you take your bearings. Your inner compass would go nuts. You would lose your way. Maybe this sounds excessive, but believe me, you have to trust the other in all things. That's where safe harbor lies.

Ten years ago, in the middle of the happiest marriage known to man, my husband, Larry, lied. It made me crazy. It made me feel lost. He, being my most solid, unshifting landmark—shifted. I lost my bearings. Home was—where? This is what happened:

He'd given up smoking his cherished Camel cigarettes. He loved the way a Camel looked, smelled, tasted, and felt between his fingers. But we also loved our life, and we both agreed to stop. We hadn't smoked for a year.

And then Larry entered a shark tournament with a couple of buddies, caught the humongous prize winner, and steamed home enfolded in a glorious haze of macho, swashbuckling congratulations from his companions. Morty, the lead macho man of the lot, offered him a cigarette, and in a bonding, male-ritual kind of Marlboro Man moment, Larry took the damn cigarette—and fell off the wagon. Feverishly, he smoked the rest of the fishing weekend; smoke, smoke, smoke, he couldn't inhale fast enough.

Wait. That wasn't the terrible part. Who among us hasn't ever fallen off a wagon? The terrible part about it was that he kept it a secret. It took me five minutes to find out. When you learn to trust a landmark, if it suddenly looks funny, you can always tell. I knew he was due to return to our own marina on Sunday, and wanting to surprise him, I drove up to the dock as he was climbing off the *Sherry J.*

He spotted me. Then I caught him making the most imperceptible, *furtive* movement. When you know someone's body language and he makes even a slight *hiding* gesture—

it's as clear as if you saw it written on his forehead in Magic Marker. Every clue in his face, his expression, his body movement, shrieks out, *"I'm not telling you something!"*

What Larry was doing, of course, was ditching the cigarette he was ashamed to tell me had, once again, seduced him. My heart sank like a stone. I saw his hand cup the cigarette in the same, familiar smoking gesture I recognized, saw him see me—then drop the thing. So what that it was only a cigarette: the very act of concealment constituted a lie. What happened to perfect trust? If he could hide one thing, he could . . . Oh, God.

I couldn't talk about it. I pretended I hadn't seen. It was just too terrible to embarrass him and me. For three days I felt estranged from my husband. Overreaction? Maybe. But I'd lost my bearings: I didn't know where I was in my marriage.

Then, in a rush of tears, after he'd asked a zillion times—"What's wrong? I *know* something's wrong"—I told him. And he understood perfectly: I wasn't upset that he'd temporarily strayed off course, but *only* that he'd damaged my landmark, not confided that he was smoking again.

It was an emotional moment. It was also an epiphany in our marriage: we both learned something that was core, absolutely bedrock in the nature of relationships. A ravaged landmark makes you doubt yourself, doubt your good judgment, doubt everything that *used* to be in place. Neither of us was really surprised that it took a while before perfect trust was reestablished, before I found my bearings again.

Lesson: Never lie to your significant other. You might get lost at sea.

17

DANGER

*Adventures together whet
the marital appetites.*

———— ◆ ————

Frankly, I never saw what was so compellingly interesting about challenges that involve danger. It's my deepest nature to worry. My theory has always been that every cold, before you know it, can turn into a fatal illness. Larry thinks that every fatal illness is probably a cold. I worry about being cut off in our prime. Is it almost over? I ask him regularly. How much longer do we have? Plenty long, he always says. As long as we want.

But why tempt fate? There are lots of safe places to go on vacation that are really interesting. I don't need to hike through untamed Anatolia when there's a tame but exotic camel auction in Fez. Just why would anyone take a midnight drive in falling sleet and snow when the newscasters tell you danger lurks? Why would anyone go white-water rafting? Tempting fate is dangerous.

And why not instantly flee for home when you're on the sea and the sky turns gray? Why go out at all when the weather is even a tad iffy? Why fish fifty miles out for toothy mako sharks when all those nice fluke are hanging out in the harbor? Why indeed.

Because I've come to understand (albeit reluctantly) that the point of fishing is not to get where the fish are, or even to catch the fish. It's the quest—and the chance of some risk. The spine of the experience is the possibility of an adventure. And when you make something happen that's different from the mundane, it's rousing, it brings you out of yourself; the best or maybe the most complicated parts of you come alive. A lot of it has to do with self-testing, and when you've come up proud and you've done the right thing . . . well then, you're okay. Your own reactions have become interesting to you. A soupçon of danger takes the humdrum out of the day, puts a *summons* in the air. When you love someone, sure you're nourished by peace and familiarity, but every now and then you have to surprise the other. You have to surprise yourself. When you know that you can change for the better by risking danger, why, you're almost a whole new person already.

————

It appears that all creatures who wish to change must take a risk. A growing three-pound lobster knows when he has to shed the two-pound shell in which he's feeling pretty squeezed; if he wants to survive, he must change—knock off the confining hull so that the pink membrane inside can grow into a bigger, more vital house. In the next step of the process, the lobster takes an enormous risk; temporarily unshelled, unprotected, he doesn't hide but moves farther out to sea, where he might get eaten by a larger sea creature or hit by a reef. Still, because the lobster knows instinctively he must court danger to change, he takes a chance and goes. Otherwise, in the stifling shell, he's dead before he's dead.

I used to think fishing was endlessly dull, but Larry has

taught me to watch the water for the color changes that are a road map to the never-ending vagaries of the ocean. Sudden darker areas can indicate depth or a storm coming or a killer shoal. I also know how to watch the sky for the peculiar kind of cumulus cloud that pretends to be benign but harbors the hounds of hell in a sudden summer squall. And I watch lazily for the flock of birds "working" that indicate schools of surface bait fish fleeing from the monster shark, just below.

That monster shark. Silently he slices the water with his fin, and I feel a thrill in my stomach and the most elegant, gentle tug on the end of the line. I know he's fallen in love with my gorgeous mackerel, but he hasn't yet felt the hook he's gracefully swallowed. So, then he does. And he makes such a commotion. Surging away, ripping the line off my reel, circling back, thrashing angrily, now quieting, now being a *good* shark, *niiiiice* shark, swimming in obedient circles at the end of my line, up to the very edge of the boat—not four feet from my hand.

Trust me, the shark seems to say.

Oh, sure. I'm no dummy. First of all, really cranky mako sharks have been known to jump right into the cockpit of a boat. And though it looks as though this one's going to be an easy catch, I haven't forgotten about those teeth, and I've got to pacify him so he's receptive and quiet for the gaff—a metal rod attached to a massive hook used to land these babies. I have to cool it, not panic. Sherry J. (the real one— me, not the boat) *laughs* at the swirling seas, the blood-red eye of the shark.

I'm lying through my teeth. What I am is scared silly, but I go ahead with it. Otherwise I will lose the fish—or worse, the husband's arm, which is on the other end of the gaff. The tension is palpable when you're on one end of a pole, a toothy, massive Jaws is on the other end, and your husband is planning to further irritate Jaws by plunging a large gaff into his tail so we can hoist him out of the sea and onto the gin pole.

What if all of this doesn't work? I'm very far from home and help, and we may just end up here with a major calamity.

Why am I here?

———

When it's over, and I know I haven't been a wimp, and I learned to do something new, and I'm silly with victory and the stamping out of fear, Larry hugs me with wild abandon. We have challenged the sea and each other, and we have survived.

Now, can we go home? I pretend to grump.

———

Later, much later, we make love with freshness. We feel safe and warm, but we know we have courted danger and we are exhilarated. That does something for a marriage, let me tell you. As long as we don't have to court danger tomorrow or maybe for another month.

18

GOING TOO FAR

*Never take the other for granted
or push him too far.*

Taking risks in marriage is one thing.

Going too far is quite another.

While my husband is prone to venture way, way out to sea, he's not completely bonkers. Because boats have limited fuel capacities, he meticulously watches the gas gauges to make sure we'll always have enough fuel to get home—and then some. If we push our luck, go too far—we run out of gas and we're in trouble.

___

Workaholics who leave little time for each other also run out of gas, go too far. Everything seems all jaunty-jolly, the career is fascinating, there's a little money in the bank, each goes his own way, until suddenly, one morning, both wake up and at least one thinks, Who *are* you?

In the evening, when Larry walks through the door, my word processor gets turned off—even if I'm in the middle of writing Great Literature. On the weekends, Larry's office door stays shut, even if he's in the middle of the Trial of the Century.

___

People also go too far when they take each other for granted, when they believe that what was entrancing five years ago keeps its magical allure. Oh, no. We pay suit to each other, as in the first days. I have heard a well-nurtured relationship referred to as the "endless courtship." The way to endlessly court is to keep each other's attention.

There's this famous joke about the mule trainer. A guy buys an expensive mule and he sends for the world-famous mule trainer to teach him how to handle it. First thing the trainer does when he arrives is to take a big club from his satchel, and *whop!*—he bops the mule over the head.

"Are you *crazy?*" asks the guy. "Why did you bop my expensive mule over the head?"

"First," says the mule trainer, "you have to get his attention."

First *and* last, and in between, you have to get the other's attention—and pull it back when it falters. Larry and I provoke each other with humor. We challenge each other on books, movies, and plays. We sometimes take courses together and play devil's advocate when talking about them. We capture each other's attention by pointing out things— and then disagreeing about the things' hidden meanings, appearance, and worth to the world. If Larry is interested in talking about Chaucerian Middle English, I give him my attention because, well—even if Chaucerian Middle English sounds like the drag of the world, if it has quickened his thoughts, it must be worth my own notice.

We capture each other's attention by seeing the world through each other's eyes. Sometimes, separated at a crowded party, we search out each other's glances and, without speaking, know exactly what funny thing the other is thinking—and then, mystifying our companions of the moment, we each laugh out loud from our separate corners of the room. Sometimes, out to dinner with insufferably boring people, I mercilessly pinch and prod Larry under the table: he knows I'm saying, "Get the check or else I'll get *you* later!"

We try to keep each other *stirring*—intellectually, humorously, sexually, emotionally. We never assume that because once we were all things to each other, it will always be so: we have to tend the relationship.

———

People who don't tend to themselves as well as to the relationship also go too far. Individually we work hard to stretch our own minds, get excited about new things, keep our bodies strong, find new ways to feel powerful.

We go too far when bitter silences are etched in stone. We must keep our communication open—even when we feel terribly angry. When once we fall into the habit of not talking, it is so easy to make silence the norm.

We go too far when we're too ambitious for the other, when we can't tolerate the other's failure. If one botches a job, even out of carelessness, the other must try to remember how it feels to screw up and then hold the other and tell him, It's all right, honey, everything will be fine.

People go too far when they test each other's devotion too harshly. I know Larry would give up his profession, his friends, his life's blood, for me if for some crazy reason I truly needed him to do that. But once, in a moment of perversity, I asked him if he'd consider giving up fishing for me.

Fishing is Larry's essence. It makes him feel free. Five hours of feeling the tide tug at the boat's keel is a spiritual experience, a health spa, his own Walden Pond, Pilgrim Creek, and *Old Man and the Sea* wrapped up in one. While I'm endlessly looking for a billboard midsea with a purple neon sign flashing BIGGEST * FLOUNDER * LIVE * HERE * IN * THIS * SPOT, he's happily trying to figure out where he would swim if he were a fish. When I'm looking at my watch—my, how time flies when we're having fun, it's *only* 9:00 A.M.?—he's already planning next weekend.

So when I asked him if he'd give up fishing, he hesitated—too long. The moment passed.

———

That night I dreamed of Larry with his *new*, much younger, awfully cute wife gazing up at him adoringly. He's got their new baby strapped to his chest (at *his age? yes!*). They're standing on the deck of *our* boat, renamed the *Janice R.*

SHE WENT TOO FAR, reads the marital epitaph.

19

WHERE HOME IS

Home is safe harbor for all the family—even if
they kick up a storm there.

The water is flat calm when we leave the dock, cobalt blue, the sun shooting diamonds into the sea. Ah, me, just thee and me, two decades after our first date, minus the white piqué sundress and plus the number-fifteen sun guard, *if* I remember. Lazy, hazy fishing day.

But the wind coming from the south on the South Shore of Long Island is fast and furious and unexpected. Spring is the treacherous, wildest wind time, defenses are down, I always forget, damn. Got to keep those defenses up always, that's my mom's lesson, don't trust anything or anybody. The murderous spring wind whips the benign ocean into a roiling salt cauldron. We get caught.

Oh! Now, every thirty seconds, ice waves come, slapping us in the face, pouring down our necks, making us gasp with shock. Sometimes we take eight waves, not too bad, only the violent sensation of the bow hitting cement, but no freezing water in the face—and then the ninth wave smashes our noses and our eyes and our cheeks and foreheads and leaves us speechless. Whenever I'm not looking (the story of my life), a wall of water comes up to slam me in the face.

Larry insists upon driving the boat from the open fly-bridge, where the visibility is better, even though I plead with him to take the wheel in the cabin down below. I know he's going to have a heart attack. *I'm* having a heart attack.

"You go down to the cabin," he shouts over the blare of the wind. "I don't need you up here."

Oh, yes, he does. He *needs* my whimpering, my terror, my directions—"Do this, do that, go faster, get us *out* of here!" He needs that badly. But he doesn't know it: he, who attends to me deeply on shore, here ignores me totally. I am a fly on his noggin. Less. I lash us together with the strap from the life preserver: if the boat is to go over, we go together. I'd rather be in the wild ocean with him than alone on this damned boat.

What I really want him to do is go another way. This much I know: If he doesn't buck the wind, the battering will stop. Then the boat won't split apart in a zillion fragments, our lives won't end, the cold slaps will cease, the . . .

Shhhh, he says. Be quiet.

I can't believe it. He never tells me to be quiet.

I will *not* be quiet.

But Larry knows the way home. He keeps his eye on the goal. He has his Loran, his compass, his inner radar. His eyes don't move from the target. He is strong and focused and steady. He will not deviate from the course.

I'd deviate all over the place to stop the punishment. *Now.* I like instant gratification. But he, surefooted on the sea, knows that roughness doesn't kill you. He will not panic. No matter how much *I* panic, berate him, plead with him, he will not be convinced. He is a sweet man, but immovable when he's convinced he's right. And he's certain, he says later, all he has to do is keep going slowly, *endure*, and he will get us home. He knows where home is. He won't go anywhere else.

———

Months later, Adam, sixteen, is blind with anger at us. It is 4:00 A.M., he has been to a party and forgotten to call to tell us he'd be late. When he finally appears, I'm there—me—his mom—waiting to remind him of his lack of consideration, his lack of attention to his SATs, and in case he hadn't noticed, nine other things he hasn't done right. Kid *explodes* his teen spleen. He has *had* it with this family, we treat him like a baby, he *hates* us, he is out of here. And he grabs his jacket and starts for the door. I try to stop him, stand in his way. He roughly pushes me aside.

I am speechless. Angry. I am also a modern mother. He knows better than to *touch* me with fury. We deal in words in this family, not brute strength. We're literate, sophisticated, read Bettelheim. Modern parents don't use force: I'll have to let him go. Besides, he's five inches taller than I. We've taught him to make his own, responsible decisions. He wants to run out in the middle of the night in a blind fury, smash up the car, get into God knows what kind of trouble— we have to let him. Oh, God, I'm going to die from terror, but we have to let this child run out of our door, into the night.

Oh, no, we don't. Larry keeps his eye on the target, and the target is home. We must settle our furies—here, now, at *home.* There will be no running away. Teenage rebellion doesn't scare my husband. "I hate you" rolls off his shoulder.

You don't die from rough going. Endure. Larry blocks the door with his body.

We love you, we will talk, he says. But you may not leave. May *not*. This to a man-child.

Facedown.

Steam comes out of our man-child's ears.

And then he storms up to his room. The next day we have it out.

———

The next decade he asks his father to be best man at his wedding. Eye on the target. Home. Endure. Steady. Rough waters won't kill you. You can make it through.

20

NO ONE'S PERFECT

Try not to try to change him.

~

We're really very different.

I'm fast. Move it! Grab the edge, just *do* it—don't think so much.

You *have* to think before you act, Larry declares. Grabbing the edge can cut you, he gets out just before the pillow I throw at his head connects.

He's deliberate (read *poke*), waits his turn, never slinks into the front for a better view of the parade even when I've already edged out seven parade revelers who weren't paying attention.

I read five books to Larry's one. Ten minutes after I've turned the last page of a play, I might not be able to tell you the protagonist's name. Larry remembers every minor character plus the stage directions.

He likes a conflicting idea, a pal who will affectionately wrangle with him, stretch his imagination, enrich his view. I love it when people say what I already think.

He always tells the truth. I always tell the truth, also—to Larry. I tell the truth to everyone else as well, but to everyone else, sometimes I don't tell all of it.

Fishing gives Larry permission to stop the serious wrangling his business requires and even to stop all affectionate wrangling for a while; fishing gives him permission just to *be*. At sea he is deaf to calls, except that of the crazy loon. At sea he is removed from phone calls, court calls, people-in-trouble calls, losses, and scores.

Fishing gives me permission to push for the prize, yet another landscape in which to score.

The waves are building, I want to plow right through, get home faster than the speed of light, but Larry maddeningly steers the bow at an angle to the waves: this guides us somewhat away from safe harbor. In the long run, he explains, it may take more time, but it's easier on the boat and easier on us if we don't take the pounding.

I'll take the pounding, attack the angry sea, only find me my home port fast.

It is my nature to *respond*, to act impulsively, to write angry letters to editors of newspapers. Larry's angry letters are confined to his business.

Not a perfect match of personalities, one would think. One would be correct. So what? It works.

It works every place except when it comes to family relations, where, unfailingly, I am stuck in the role of The Heavy and my husband is Larry, The Nonconfrontational.

Look, what gets me angriest is that Larry is plenty confrontational in court, where face-off clashes are his best subject. Adversaries know better than to try to take advantage of him, colleagues admire his challenges, and clients rest easy under his guard. But when it comes to family, Larry's penchant for peace at all costs has often been a bone of contention, and it got worse as our children grew. He was outrageously unwilling to stick up for me when they were being outrageous. In our house, did one ever hear "Cut it out, Jennifer, don't *do* that, Adam, Mom's *right*"?

No. Just didn't happen.

I wanted him to be on my team, no matter what. He refused to choose sides.

Even Dr. Spock said he should choose sides, my side. Didn't happen. In Larry's defense, he'd never join *their* team, either: he just wouldn't play the game.

I know he's on my side, I know he always chooses me over anyone else in our family, he just won't do it out loud. He doesn't make a point of sticking up for me.

The first time it happened began a true danger period for our relationship. We were married just a few weeks, and at the time his mother was neither wise nor kind. As the years passed she became my firm advocate, and I hers, but in the beginning it was difficult.

"So what are *you* going to do to help our children financially?" she asked my mom and dad one evening after she'd given us a gift. "If I were you, I'd have put money aside for a rainy day—then you'd be able to do your share for this young couple. I believe in doing the right thing."

I saw my parents grow small. All their lives they'd been working hard and denying their own pleasures to make sure I had books, went to camp, went to college, had a prom gown, had a pretty wedding.

They didn't answer my husband's mother. They just kept quiet. I think a part of them even agreed with her—some atavistic guilt made them believe she had a point. They also were nonconfrontational.

I, however, wanted to tear my husband's mother apart.

How dare she hurt my parents? I looked over at my new husband, my knight in shining armor.

Nothing. He said nothing.

Then the knight changed the subject. "Let's eat," he said.

I wanted to tear *him* apart.

Later, at home, I did.

"Why didn't you defend them? How could you remain silent? I hated you!"

"Do what I do—ignore her," he said. "She means no harm."

But he didn't say he'd tell her to stop. And he didn't.

"How can you be so damned passive? Is it your mother or me?" I'd ask in disbelief and anger.

"It's you, you—always you," he'd answer quietly. "But I just won't yell at her."

I saw his family passivity as a terrible flaw. When others savaged me, I sought to be avenged by Larry.

What was sought remained unfound.

———

I was desperate. One day, after a particularly hurtful moment, I wondered if his nature had anything in common with others who fished. I remember taking down Larry's very worn copy of Izaak Walton's *Compleat Angler*, opening the book to a random page, and there it was—a message from the year 1653:

"Anglers are quiet men . . . of mild and sweet and peaceable spirits," wrote the ancient fisherman.

Tell me about it, Izaak. Then I pulled down Dame Juliana Berners's *The Treatise of Fishing with an Angle*, the earliest known writing on the subject of sportfishing: written in 1421, it predates Izaak Walton by more than two hundred years. Dame Juliana was a nun who loved to reel in a fat one.

"If a man wishes to be always in merry thoughts, and have a glad spirit," said ace angler Dame Juliana, "he must avoid quarrelsome company and places of dispute."

They had my husband's number—these two ancient fisherfolk. They understood.

Leave the guy alone. He doesn't have to be all things to you.

————

I had to face that it is Larry's profound nature not to be angry, accusatory, or confrontational with people he loves. In the courtroom, he confronts. At home, he won't. This may not be the nature of all fishermen, but it's true of *my* fisherman. I could take it or leave it, but I couldn't change him. And if I kept trying to change him, I would grow sour.

I took it.

For true intimacy, love a real person, not a whitewashed version of the person, not a fiction constructed from self-serving fantasies. I no longer try to combine us into a single personality, two biographies becoming one. We have different histories even if we share the same future.

Now I fight my own family battles. When he withdraws from them, I try to understand, try to flow with his tide as he does so often with mine. He is what he is—a man of peaceable spirit.

————

No one's perfect.

21

CHANGING THE SUBJECT

Can you divert him from a heavy heart?
Better learn how.

———

Sometimes the spirit is heavier than lead. The word *heart-ache* takes on new meaning: my heart really aches, the pain is palpable, my chest is so sore. I take two aspirin. It doesn't help.

I can't breathe, I'm not sure I want to breathe. I can't stop crying. How can a cherished kinship go suddenly sour? This grief is about betrayal, misunderstanding, loss, and cruelty: I think I will have to live with it every moment of the rest of my life. Screams of pain and rage fly inside me like bats.

I can't give up my sorrow, don't want to give it up. Want to wallow in it. Want him to wallow in it with me.

But no. We have to go fishing.

"It'll do you good," says my husband. "Come with me today. I want you to come with me."

I want to stay home and fixate on my loss, but I relent and get in the car for the drive to the boat.

I'm silent all the way. Isn't marriage about tearing yourself up if the other is torn up? Larry is changing the subject, the subject that's consuming me, and I resent it.

Today, it appears, we're going for blues. I stare glumly at the boat wake as we make our way to deeper water. Larry lets the lines out, and the baits skip along in the wake: I am immune to baits, salt, sky, sea, and the whole radiant, restless day. I hold my grief tight.

All of a sudden the water boils and seethes with the lightning movement of bait fish. Silver menhaden pursued by the violent bluefish make wild leaps into the air. What terror they must feel to be induced to leave the comfort of their sea for suffocating air. Nasty gulls screech sound effects, and the sea tumbles with drama.

Who cares. I want to concentrate on betrayal.

Larry thrusts a rod into my hands, and in an instant it's almost ripped from me. A hit! Reluctantly I'm involved.

The blue dives down deep. I can't give him an ounce of slack because he'll use it to shake the hook or cut the line with his brutal teeth. I brace my legs to meet the rolling of the boat, yank the rod hard to set the hook in his mouth, and then it's just the fish and me.

Off he rushes to China, tearing the hissing line from the reel. Steady, steady, if I let the tautness go, the line will break or tangle and he'll bolt free.

The blue plunges for even deeper water, his safe place; then up to the surface he soars, and I get a glimpse of his flashing, flailing tail. Repeatedly he leaps from the water, shakes his head like a terrier, disgorges his stomach contents like the old Roman banqueters, and dives down deep again. It is a savage show. Good. I feel savage.

This fish is alive. It is mean. It requires my deepest

attention. My own heart beats so quickly, I feel I'm also on the hook.

It is the fish or me, all my despair suddenly concentrated on that small, ferocious body. I am ferocious in the catching.

It takes fifteen minutes. Suddenly I hurl him aboard, and Larry yells, "Great! He's a beauty—lunch!"

———

He's more than lunch. I don't feel one bit sorry for the thumping fish in the fish box. The worst of my anger and grief has been caught there, in the cold, mysterious eyes of the bluefish.

22

KNOTS

*Let the lines out: unravel the knots that
choice relationships.*

___

My own mother always assumed that motherhood gave her
privileges, gave her rank.

"Tell me everything—I'm your *mother.*"

"To a *mother* you talk that way?"

"Who do you think will tell you the truth about how
awful that looks on you? Only your mother."

Motherhood lay weighty on my mother.

___

Motherhood jitterbugs inside me. I love Jennifer and Adam,
love their free spirits, love their spouses, Steve and Sue
(*moi*—a *mother-in-law?* a kid like me? impossible!), love the
notion that Larry and I will have *lineage.* And, it appears, my
kids talk any way they wish to me.

Despite our different approaches, there is, if you want
to know the truth, something very deep inside that believes
my mother as to the power of the mother/child relationship.
Who else would really die for Jen and Adam? Only me. And
they know it.

Wrong. They know nothing of the sort. And even if
they believed it, they wouldn't care. I'm the last person with

whom they share intimacies, and it's not even because they
fear seeing themselves in print. Well, that, too, but mostly
they don't tell me secrets because they know that only their
spouses, only Steve and Susan, could truly understand.

———

When Adam was small, I thought I owned him, little
browned body setting out his lobster pots, skimming the
harbor in his Boston Whaler (you could cut it in half and it
wouldn't sink, say the ads—my kind of boat). I suffered for
him at Little League, wanted to tear out the throat of the
coach who dumped him in basketball, cheered for him at
track, lost him once when he was three and literally could not
breathe until his sister found him.

When he was a little boy, I think he believed we were
people of infinite psychological resources, perfect solutions.
Those were the days. We fished, the four of us—at least
Larry and Adam fished: Jen and I mostly soaked up rays. Talk
about togetherness. Steady, predictable tides swept us forward, steady family ties.

Adam grew up, off he went to Dublin to study James
Joyce, tend bar in a pub, clean fish in Alaska, and—what is
this?—all of a sudden I didn't own him anymore. Own him?
I was lucky if he slept home once in six months, trashing the
house with his laundry. What's more, I could be the guru of
perfect solutions, the Buddha of infinite resources, he wasn't
having any of it.

Tonight he sits in our living room, so blue-eyed, so
radiant, so strong—I could burst. For years I'd been hoping
that he'd marry Susan, lovely, wise architect of buildings and
feelings—my friend. Finally he did.

His elegant new wife shares a secret smile with him. They laugh out loud.

I look at my son—flesh of my flesh—and what? *What? What are you thinking*, God damn it? He'll never tell me.

Okay—what's so funny? What did I miss?

Oh, Mom, he says sweetly. Back off. It's private. Private? From a mother? Apparently.

So now I know how my own mother feels; and *that* was never supposed to happen.

———

It's the same with Steven, Jen's husband. Steve and I share boat boredom, wry humor, and a lust for carrot soup. He's a master of trends: I like to hear what's going to happen next; he always knows. We love disagreeing on what's hot and what's not. He prodded me, kicking and screaming, into the new world when he insisted that my children buy me a word processor for my birthday. I don't need a word processor, I said, teeth clenched. Yes, you do, he told me. I hate it, I said. You won't, he answered.

What we don't share is Jennifer. *He's* got her.

How is it that this woman, flesh of my flesh, gentles to *his* voice—okay, it's one of those fabulous radio voices—and she bristles to mine, a so-wise mother voice? We had the usual adolescent mother/daughter angst (maybe a tad worse than usual), but I thought she was tied to me, inexorably. Deep down we were the same person in a way.

If we're so much the same, how is it that this child of mine switched allegiances *just like that!* It's Steve, Steve, Steve, and Steve yet again. It's Sue, Sue, Sue, and Sue yet again. Back off, Mom. Lighten up, Mom. I don't care to tell you, Mother.

It appears that on the lines that link us with our children, knots inevitably must appear—knots of lost loyalties, misunderstandings, even swift and sudden rages. Knots in the stomach.

———

"Knots" is a nautical term. It means the speed at which you move in your boat, the number of nautical miles you travel per hour. Knots are also vital when you fish because a good knot keeps the hook on the line. Fishermen respect the intricacies of good knots so much, they even lovingly name them: Larry spends you would not believe how many hours reading about the vagaries of the Beautiful Bimini Twist.

But, occasionally, the fishing line itself twists into an unwanted knot. Big trouble. When a line develops even one puny knot, you have to let it out, free the line until you reach the knot—even if it's at the end of a three-hundred-foot reel. There's no way to undo the trouble when the line is taut and the knot is hidden under spirals of other line. But with the line loosened, you can unravel the knot. It takes time and patience to free the line, let that endless mess out into the sea and slowly reel it back until it's smooth and knotless. If you ignore even a tiny knot, hoping it will smooth out by itself as you reel up your monster codfish, the line breaks or tangles and you're dead—and the monster codfish is alive and well.

———

The lines that bind us to children are powerfully strong, but they weaken if the knots on those lines remain a snarled mess. To loosen the knots, we've got to let the line out—all the way.

There comes a time, damn it, when parents must let go

of the happy view that we, like General Haig, are in control here.

Lines loosened and let out, relationships grow smoother, but inexorably the space between us grows. We've even lost our boating crew. Our children's spouses make feeble attempts to share sea enthusiasm with us, but I haven't noticed one of the four of them down at the dock this season.

What do I expect—that's what we taught them to do, reminds Larry. That's what it's like to be well married, reminds Larry; sometimes it's tough on everyone else who loves you. We're exactly like that with *our* parents, reminds Larry.

Oh, shut up, Larry.

23

WEATHERING THE
STORMS

A good laugh tames a tempest. If you're
not funny, get funny.

We were on our way, *not* to the boatyard, for a change, but to see my pal in summer stock. When we *are* on our way to the boatyard, Larry drives like the wind. On the way to summer stock, he dreamed, idled, poked along. And then he stopped totally—even though the light was green—to let the little old lady make her way, painfully, slowly, across the street. The cabdriver behind us leaned on his horn in the inimitable manner of cabdrivers all over the world, and he also threw in some creative finger gestures, in case we missed his point.

"You could have gone around the lady," I hissed to Larry. Conflict makes me nervous.

And then I watched with amazement as Larry, clearly born wearing glasses and thin as a reed, gently turned off the engine, took his car keys, opened his door, and walked back to the taxi.

Oh, God, a fight, I thought, slinking down on my seat with terror and embarrassment.

Poised for flight, with one eye on the re* the other on the door, I saw Larry offer cabdriver, and miracle of miracles, I saw th shoulders begin to heave with laughter as h in mock despair.

"What happened?" I asked when Larry came back.

"I handed him the keys," said Larry, "and told him, 'Here—you run her over. I haven't the heart.' "

———

God, I love a man who can make me laugh. Larry has a way of defusing conflict by breaking me up with humor. I can't do it nearly as well as he, but I've been working on being funny. It's the world's most effective tool for weathering the storms. Once, when Larry had been acting kind of autocratic the night before, I propped at his place at the breakfast table the book entitled *Hitler, a Study in Tyranny*. I got a lot of credit for that one.

And once, when Larry and a sailing friend came in *hours* after they said they'd be home, I wanted to *kill* them both: instead, having listened to their lame excuses, I told the two of them to do me a favor and just tack off—we all laughed at my superior wit, and what could have been an ugly moment passed.

When I was younger, I steered a 180 degree course away from conflict. I didn't see how a couple could find its way out of a really heavy disagreement. But now that I've honed my funny skills, I've come to understand that a marriage can grow through conflict if one doesn't diminish the other, if each partner is able to maintain a certain autonomy, a sense of personal authority and importance and equality. I feel so safe in marriage because the strong part of me is epted: even when we disagree, I feel connected. I know Larry doesn't want me *vanquished*. Just, he says, a little more pliable, please. The issue with us is never defeat and conquer—and that's why I give in to his stab at humor—even when it's not really very funny. I know he's trying—and that's what counts.

———

There's scientific evidence that shared laughter is a bonding agent: just as you physically can't smile and frown at the same moment, you can't laugh and be real angry at the same time.

I just know I've gotten *much* funnier. Good thing, too, because I suspect that when we are old and gray, having weathered many storms together, we will remember the times we had each other in stitches far more vividly than we will remember the times we had each other furious or even the times when we just had each other.

24

SURRENDER

Only when you let yourself be completely vulnerable will the earth move.

Boating pleasure is totally dependent on being able to trust the captain, surrender control to the captain. So gladly, I surrender. I give it up. Get me there, get me back. I trust him wholly.

Great sex is also dependent on trust. And, as in boating, with trust comes her sister, surrender.

Surrender is a dirty word to a woman who requires control. I happen to like being master of the universe. I happen to like being in charge of my time and my emotions, not to mention what my body does and how it looks. But I know that during lovemaking, if I don't concentrate fully on the sensations of arousal, if I don't surrender the protective stances that serve me well in my master-of-the-universe mode, the earth won't move. It's as simple as that: you have to *concentrate* on body and throw modesty and control out the window—or the earth won't even quiver.

Easier said than done. It was difficult to trust Larry enough to completely surrender myself to the rhythm of the sexual dance. What if my *fat* showed, and what if my breasts didn't look quite perky, and how can you hold in your stomach and surrender at the same time? Even today I still think about these things.

It took time to understand that he simply wasn't aware of my fat or of any of the other awkward things my body did when I was homing in on sensation, when I was yielding control. He had already surrendered to love.

It was my husband's love that finally allowed me to yield. And then the sex got great. Good thing I learned: great sex with your spouse is the big payoff for monogamy.

———

When I was very young, I knew all about great sex. I knew what you *did*. But the thing I worried a lot about was what you *said*. Like, what did you say after you kissed in one of those movie clinches? What did you say after you actually did *it*? It was going to be so embarrassing, I thought.

Little did I know that surrendering to love also means the freedom to tell jokes, act lunatic, laugh yourself silly after *it*. And sometimes even during *it*. And usually before *it*. I can't imagine great foreplay without laughs: without laughs, it would be foredocudrama.

The only way you can be funny during sex is if you are totally familiar with what the other thinks is funny. If you can trust that you will know each other's reactions, you can also trust that you will know each other's hearts: you can surrender your fear of saying the wrong thing and offending your partner. Recently, in mock disgust at Larry's perpetual readiness for lovemaking, I told him he was acting like a horny teenager and being a pain in the neck and that he ought to go to Age School to learn how to be sixty. "I ought to *teach*

Age School," Larry retorted. "To paraphrase Gloria Steinem, this is what sixty acts like."

Familiarity also breeds understanding, and that's pretty helpful, especially if one partner has a sexual hang-up. Giving up your own self-consciousness, allowing yourself occasionally to surrender to the old inhibitions because you know your partner understands—well, that's deeply liberating.

Here is my sexual hang-up:

I don't know if it comes from the time when my mother told me to be careful lest sex rear its ugly head, but whatever—regularly, I forget, just forget, how good it is to make love. So then I say no.

I seem to say no a lot.

———

But here's the good news: Familiarity makes it possible for one spouse to know when the other really means no. If you truly do mean no, then the other is fine and loving about it, and she just holds you, he just holds you.

But if you say no only because you've forgotten again, well then, the other doesn't get put off, doesn't get insulted, doesn't get moody, stays in the moment, deeply romantic. Larry persists, cajoling me, humoring me, romping with me, patiently stroking me into the goodness of lovemaking. Then—well then, *I'm* able to surrender to the moment.

"Oh, thank you," I tell him. "What if I didn't remember? I would have *missed* it."

We often thank each other for swell lovemaking, by the way. It's only polite.

Not to worry, he'll always remind me, he says with a

grin. No matter how many times I forget, he'll always remind me if I want the reminding.

I want the reminding.

———

And when the earth doesn't move because sometimes I can't give it up, can't let go of the control—not to worry, he promises, tomorrow it will move. And it will. I trust that it will because I've learned not to fear surrender.

PART 4 SEA OF PLENTY

Fishing for Our Lives

25

R E N E W A L

*An occasional change of scenery makes
the show come alive!*

While everyone else is enjoying the red-and-yellow turning
of the leaves, the crisp bite in the air that signals fall, Hallow-
een, and frosty ice skaters on the lake, Larry is stubbornly
insisting we're only in the cool part of the summer. He
cannot bear to think that fishing's over for the season. Not
until after Thanksgiving and the first freeze does my husband
sadly concede defeat to nature. The engines of the *Sherry J.*
are decommissioned, and Larry snarls hello to winter.

December, January, and February snail-pace by for him,
while I engage us in an ecstasy of snow walks, museums,
theaters, and restaurants that don't serve fish.

Around the ides of March, Larry starts brightening; his
blood fairly bubbles with anticipation. The days are getting
longer, he announces, the sky is softening.

I pretend not to hear.

But he has noticed the first balmy breeze that has es-
caped everyone else's attention. He points out the green
buds on the trees, eager to unfurl into leaves, the tootling
squirrels, the yellow crocuses in Central Park peeking out of
the winter debris. Let's just take a drive to Freeport

suggests; the boatyard must be a beehive of activity, and I'd just like to check the boat.

I've heard this "beehive of activity" line before, but, kindly as I am, I pile into the car with him for the ides of March checkup, and it's never a surprise to find the boatyard still as death except for the one guy who is nuttier than the one I married, passionately simonizing the bow of his own obsession. *See?* says Larry. I *told* you.

Down come the reels from the top of the closet to be cleaned and oiled, out come the rods to be inspected for cracks, patiently I put out my two hands and act as human spool winder as he prepares the new fishing line. He's close to ecstatic. Aches and disappointments of winter disappear: Larry's renewal season is upon us.

———

It's *my* qualmish season. I know there's something called SAD, Seasonal Affective Disorder: people who need the light of summer become chemically depressed when the days are long and dark in winter. I, on the other hand, suffer from HIC, an acronym for "Here It Comes," and what's coming are the preparation rituals, the scrubbing, polishing, oiling, greasing, shining, cleaning out dry rot on the cold, cramped boat. Sure, it feels good at the end when the boat is all shiny and eager to surge, but I loathe the work.

Truth is, that's only part of it: the other part is that in contrast with the SAD people who flourish in sunlight, I _____ when spring starts, when cherry pinks _____ whites are upon us. All that loosening up, _____ ma underfoot makes me a little nervous. _____ eks I get into it, but the first days of _____ my mate undo me.

First of all, it seems to me that winter is the safer, more romantic season, so good for snuggling indoors by a fire. Or just for snuggling. The blackening sky quickens my soul and imagination, makes it easier to burrow deeper into my beloved bed with a great book. Second, because my work defines me, I always feel slightly guilty taking off in the *daytime*. As writer Laura Cunningham describes it, "The pagan and the puritan fight it out at the first sniff of chlorophyll." I'm most secure working indoors, where I'm comfy and safe, while outside it's dark, cold, and cranky and the winter storms are storming.

But work happily or stay in bed with a book when the canary-colored sun is hot and brilliant, the first whiff of salt is in the air, and the husband is restless? Impossible. For Larry's sake, every spring I fight my neurosis until the pagan wins. I go to work on the boat. I know he needs this season to renew his life force.

I've known it since my fortieth birthday, when he made it clear to me that every person, every season, every marriage, needs a regular, purposeful renewal. In October of that year, as I was beset with feelings of age coming down hard, he surprised me three hours before departure with tickets to New Orleans. For a whole weekend we listened to old-timers play hot and steamy jazz at Preservation Hall, danced on the banks of the Mississippi, worshiped at the secret grave of Marie Laveau, the voodoo queen, and ate ourselves silly with jambalaya.

The Creole natives call it lagniappe, an unexpected bonus, a serendipitous gift. The surprise trip Larry gave me gave *us* a sense of renewal. We looked at each other freshly. We felt full of beans. We *were* full of beans. The unplanned vacation, the unanticipated fun, took our marriage right back to where it began—to a sense of *anything's possible.* It made me feel like a million dollars.

I'm a fast learner. It's usually I who plan for the minitrips now, stealing a three-day weekend sometimes to travel just an hour away. It's not the great distances or even the surprise element, but the room with the different view that never fails to energize *and* calm both of us. Scenery changes breathe new flowering into our relationship.

Still, there's the inescapable truth: For Larry's perpetual bloom, he needs to be the second guy of the boating season to get those engines going. Oh, *okay*, I grump. Some beehive of activity.

26

LIFESAVERS

When the other's in trouble—
do something.

Stowed in a prominent place on our boat is the flare gun, a staple for every navigator. If the boat is in danger or you're lost at sea, you shoot up these flares and they explode in the sky. Then other boats come rushing to your aid.

Early in the nineteenth century, before the United States government appointed the Coast Guard to take over the job, tiny lifesaving shacks along the local beaches were set up: their purpose was purely humanitarian. For the love of their fellow man, unpaid volunteers manned the shacks, keeping sharp eyes out for the primitive rockets or flares that indicated a vessel in peril from a shifting sandbar or a ship already capsized in a raging storm. These local lifesavers would then man their small, sturdy craft and row *(row!)* to the rescue. They were activists. They saw a need and filled it and performed spectacular feats of seamanship in the name of love. They showed fidelity, devotion, and courage.

When they saw those flares, they *moved*.

There are other kinds of flares that signal *danger*, and these glow only in the consciousness of a loved one. Sometimes we're talking lifesaving here and sometimes spirit saving. Whatever—I've learned that the person you love should be an activist, always getting out there to take you home. Like the time I totaled the car: I was very shaken but unhurt, so sure, I could have taken a taxi home after the police came, but when I called Larry and he told me to wait right in that spot—not *budge* till he got there—well, that was so fine, so loving! When I *think* of how he flew to me and of the sensation of being rescued I had, even today I feel tears of gratitude come to my eyes.

————

Maybe ten or eleven times during the course of our long marriage, I've gotten really irked—read wild with fury—with my husband. At these times I've run away from home. My adult version of running away from home never involves more than a few city blocks, and it always involves Larry's finding me—to take me home. With a sinking, despairing heart I take off. Sound childish? It is. So what. Can I help it? No. It is one way I have of expressing a need for help.

The fact is, I love to be found. And frankly, if you want to know the truth, I suspect there's something in it for the person who rescues as well as for the one who's found—a feeling of competence, a challenge answered, a call acknowledged.

Once, I grabbed a book, left him with a chicken salad I'd made (in a happier mood, earlier that day) for our dinner, and stalked out of the apartment. Six blocks away was an Indian restaurant, and I took a window seat for my lonely dinner. Why a window seat? You figure it out.

He found me. In between the mulligatawny and the curry, I looked over my book to see him grinning at me through the glass, looking lovable and tolerant of my regression into adolescence. Another time I jumped ship angrily to browse in the local bookstore, and sure enough, in about an hour, he hugged me from behind in the poetry section. How can a person stay angry?

I totally expect him to row out and find me, irrational as that is. Secretly, that's why I never go too far—only to those places he'd figure on my going. You want always to know that the person you need needs you and will get to where you are, no matter where you are in the world . . . but you have to be reasonable.

Larry doesn't need to get found as regularly as I. Still, I *know* I'm his lifesaver, and I have to be alert to those flares. Recently, in a strange city, his work going hard, he called in the evening and sounded so low. In an hour, my own work dropped, I was on a plane headed to him: our hotel room reunion was lovely, even though I'd just seen him the day before.

———

This lifesaver business is also important when you're dealing with children. Sometimes you get it wrong: you do what you think makes them feel secure, but they get another message.

Feeling as I do about always knowing there's someone there for you, I loved to read to my kids from *Are You My Mother?*, my favorite little children's book. This little bird, I think it was, gets lost, and he keeps running into animal mothers of different breeds—a cow mother, a dog mother, a hen mother—and each one he asks, "Are you my mother?" Naturally the answer is no—until he finds his real mother, the bird mother, who welcomes him lovingly and warmly within her forever maternal, forever loving, forever *there* embrace. I thought it was an adorable story, and it showed a little one how his mother would always be there for him.

Unfortunately, my daughter informed me just a while ago that she *hated, despised, was terrorized* by that story.

"The mother," said Jennifer, "got lost. She was *not* always there at all. This tiny bird had to ask a zillion people if they were his mother. They never were. Why wasn't she out looking for *him?* By the time he found the mother bird, he was *exhausted.* I had *nightmares* about that awful story."

Now Jennifer has her own little boy named Josh. He's too small to understand anything, you'd think, but Jennifer knows better. Over and over she reads him Margaret Wise Brown's *The Runaway Bunny*, who threatens *his* mom that he plans to run away, whereupon she tells him she'll run right after him.

"If you run after me," says the bunny, "I'll become a fish in a trout stream and I will swim away from you."

"If you become a fish in a trout stream," says his mother, "I will become a fisherman and I will fish for you."

"If you become a fisherman," says this bunny, testing, always testing, they all always do, "I will become a rock on the mountain, high above you."

This mother bunny is tireless about always rescuing her child, no matter how annoyingly recalcitrant he gets. He never has to go looking for her because she will always find him. She's a mover and a shaker, a lifesaver mother bunny.

My small grandson listens raptly. He seems to understand and be comforted. It's a sweet sight, the two dark heads bent low, reading about being in trouble and being found.

———

Okay, okay—I get it. Like those long-ago volunteer lifesavers, it's necessary to move swiftly and surely when someone needs you. In stormy seas, a beloved should always come to take you home.

27

SO, WHAT DO YOU THINK?

*When you marry your best friend, the talk
never grows old, the sex never grows cold.*

Trolling for striped bass with nice, clean lures, Larry doesn't
have to fool with disgusting fish tidbits, so we have time to
ruminate and see where our wandering talk takes us. The
undulating water is relaxing. Gentle waves breaking on our
bow sound deep, oceanic notes and act as background music.
It's a good day for talk. Best friends need to sound each other
out. It is the life blood of our marriage.

There's got to be something about the element of water that
inspires conversation.

Any water. I also notice the tendency to talk/talk/talk
in the locker room at the Y pool where I swim. Carol, Susan,
Laura, Lisa, Betsy, our den mother, Eleanor—each of us is an
expert in something the other needs, each of us nurtures and
shares, each takes part in the no-holds-barred intimacy of
women who meet just for the half hour it takes to strip for
the swim and dress after the swim—and still manage to
reveal the unrevealable.

I don't know what happens in the guys' locker room: I've heard that men compare instead of share—whether it's a surreptitious appraisal of each other's penis size or an open declaration of their own business smarts. Over on the women's side, though, shaking the water from our ears, relaxed from the forced meditation that thirty-six monotonous laps inspires, we don't seem to compete in our business lives, and certainly we don't even see each other's naked, imperfect bodies—some with pert bosoms, some with pendulous bosoms: our aim at the Y pool is to *un*bosom our souls, to connect and share.

The pity is that so many of these women don't believe that men can be the loyal, forthcoming, and permanent best friends they've found in each other. They're the generation of AIDS, they're the children of impermanence: their sense is that True Love is not durable. They seem to be looking for something more passionate than friendship.

There is nothing more passionate than friendship.

When Larry and I first formed our notions of True Love, things were different. AIDS were kids who got to clap erasers for the teacher. The bottom line was what you had to keep on when you practiced penmanship. Grass was mowed, not smoked, Coke cost a nickel, horse was what the Lone Ranger rode on, pot was for making chicken soup, and junkie was stuff that was made in Japan. Pasta meant spaghetti. Pasta sauce was ketchup. Take-out was what you did with the dog or the garbage.

Betty Friedan was, thank God, growing up angry, somewhere far away. And we read poetry to our boyfriends, talked, talked, talked tirelessly with them.

"You're married over thirty years—and you still *sleep* to-gether? You still *talk*—what's left to talk *about?*" one young woman at the Y ask me.

What's left? Everything. With the world changing as fast as our own lives move forward, backward, sideward, in a kaleidoscope of new events, we do not take understanding for granted. Although I have a pretty good idea of what makes Larry tick, I can't take him for granted, I can't bank on it that I'll intuitively know what he thinks, needs, wants. I have to ask him his feelings—then listen carefully to the answer. And, you better believe it, vice versa. I *hate* to be taken for granted.

If you put in the time to make talking a habit, I tell the young woman, if you marry your best friend instead of your live-in lover with whom you share furniture, rent, but rarely confidences, you've got a good chance at permanence. If you don't invest *forever* into your mind-sets, it won't work.

When you marry your real pal, the talk never grows old, the sex never grows cold.

So, one morning, I'm doing my thirty-six boring laps, the sunlight filtering through the window dapples the pool water, I'm in a trance, if it wasn't for the chlorine, this could be Bermuda, my mind swims idly all over the place—and *I have it!* I know what I want for our epitaph.

I was recently struck, while reading the memoirs of the travel writer Jan Morris, by her description of the already inscribed joint tombstone she'll share with her companion of many years. It reads:

TWO FRIENDS AT THE END OF ONE LIFE.

Perfect. I'm glad that's settled. I'm going to steal it for us.

28

FLIRTING

*"Go play," our mothers told us. Who would
have thought that playing was
the ultimate sex technique?*

There is sensuality in the sea. If there weren't, I'd figure out
a way to make it be.

I shut my eyes to the chum and the fish gurry that
irretrievably digs into the seams of the boat, and what's left
on magic summer days is rhythmic rocking, hot sun beating
on browned, almost naked bodies (even fiftyish bodies look
good with tans, and damn the dermatologists), languor, salty
mouths. Not bad. It's one thing to be alone with a lover/
husband at a movie, a tennis court, a resort—alone with a
cast of thousands: a very different thing it is to be alone on
a heaving ocean, a cast of two as far as the eye can see.
Quality time, world-divorced.

Aside from the togetherness, there really is something
erotic about the sea itself and fish, too: both have long been
associated with sex.

In ancient India, for example, the fish was always a
symbol of reproductive potency, and today suggestive fish
figures are still ubiquitous in Indian art and sculpture.

Greek fishermen worshiped Pan, the sexy goat-man

who was a god of animals and of the sea, along with Priapus, the god of sexual excitement.

Egyptians also link the sea with sexuality. In a dog-eared volume in Larry's library called *Fishing from the Earliest Times*, the Greek biographer Plutarch writes that when the Egyptian god Osiris was killed by Typhon, the god of storms, Isis, the goddess of fertility, found all of her beloved's remains except for his ill-fated penis, which had been thrown into the Nile and eaten by eels. Isis erected an obelisk to honor the lost phallus, and to this day, Egyptians observe a festival in honor of Osiris' watery manhood.

Cupid has often been painted holding a rose and a fish as symbols of love—one prickly, the other untamable.

In Naples, *pesce* is dialect for the male organ.

Medieval Greek and Roman philosophers wrote of fish as an aphrodisiac and reported it as a staple at every wedding dinner.

So there is historical precedence for sexual association with the sea. But I'd do without the history, if I had to. All by myself, somehow, I'd find fishing a sexy thing.

If you think this translates into Larry and me rolling around in spontaneous, orgiastic pleasure on the boat deck, think again. All it means is that an occasional wet, salty kiss, a well-timed thigh stroke (*not* when the line is screaming with a hooked tuna), promises *later*. That's all it takes. Anticipation and the building of excitement. Not only wouldn't I have the ghost of a chance for Larry's immediate attention to sexual intimacy when the fish are biting, but I wouldn't even sit in, let alone relax into, ecstasy on our fishy deck before it's been scrubbed to pristine sweetness. It's *later* on which I'm working.

I'm here to tell you that most well-married people don't hang around waiting for sudden moods of dizzying passion to strike as soon as they get into bed. Dizzying, spontaneous passion is swell but rare after a reasonable number of years. The wild sex of our infant marriages metamorphoses into the falling-asleep-on-the-chair-with-the-book-open position, unless we put in time making way for intimacy.

Because the fact is that great sex needs play that is very different from traditional foreplay. True sexual intimacy is a fine art requiring many cultivated skills, the most crucial being the ability to relax and have fun together. For us, playing together at boating and fishing and sunning stimulates other appetites. Play has turned out to be the consummate flirting technique.

Flirting with someone—even someone you've known for a very long time, even someone who knows you as well as one person can ever know another—is very flattering to the flirtee. And getting a positive reaction to your flirting—well, that's a real turn-on.

You'll be pleased to hear that playtime doesn't have to revolve around fishing; it could be brushing hips as you both reach for the sauce at the supermarket. It could be the noon break you've taken to schlep uptown just to have lunch in the diner with him. It could be the rhinoceros nose you hid in his briefcase before he left for the office. It could even be the kidding around at stoplights as you jog together. You're setting the stage for *later*, for premeditated lovemaking.

Some of my friends still wait only for spur-of-the-moment, unpremeditated sex. Too often the wait is endless. I believe that sex should be meditated, that each woman is responsible for her own orgasms and for keeping sexual attraction alive.

Intimacy consists in allowing yourself sexual feelings all day long. Being aroused from time to time during the day is as natural as laughing at something funny and getting on with business after the joke. It doesn't matter, either, if arousal starts with your own fantasies or from fleeting encounters with your lover during the day: whatever its source, if you *bring home the excitement*, you've got it made.

So the myth of the magic moment is largely just that—a myth. We make our own magic. We put out feelers for *later*. *Even* while we're fishing—that legendary sport of lovers. Keep your flowers and fine wine: we've got salt kisses. Sweaty hugs.

29

JUST DO IT

*The confidence of a mate is "The Gift
of the Magi."*

~

1972.

A husband, two healthy children, a house, an Airedale, a boat, and a teaching career. She Who Has It All. Placid is my middle name. I sprawl, lizardlike, on the deck, just me and the sea. I drowse.

As the sky darkens and the first raindrops fall, my watch reads 11:20 A.M. and I am counting my blessings. By noon I know we are dead ducks. Now the sky is licorice, the waves are socking the stern, I'm counting my failures.

"I forgot to write a book!" I wail over the wind to Larry. "No one ever asked for my autograph."

Then we survive the storm.

One week later, sunny, easy day on Long Island Sound, eight keepers, one throwback, Larry puts down his fishing rod and grabs my shoulders.

"Stop working," he says. "Write the book. We'll manage. It's not written in stone that you have to be a teacher forever. Reconstitute your life. Just *do* it. You *have* to do it.

No question about it, you *can* do it. It's not too late."

Such a gift that is to me. The black sky and the storm didn't frighten him last week, but my regret did. I'll never forget this present—his true faith in me.

1974. The mailman delivers a tiny package—the one I've been waiting for. I sit down on the front steps, open it slowly, and pull out the thin, canary-yellow-covered book. It reads *Tough Gazoobies on That* by Sherry Suib Cohen; it's my masterpiece, my treasure, my claim to immortality. It has my picture in it. You could drop it, you could stamp on it, it won't break. A *book*. I wrote it. In one hundred years someone will be browsing in a dusty bookshop, will spot the fading, yellow cover, buy it, take it home, read *my* thoughts from another time, another place.

I'm rushed by Adam, age twelve, who has run all the way up the block to the house.

"Look, Ads," I announce proudly, "Mom's first book."

"Great!" he shouts. "Do you have any string for my lobster pots?"

Things I'd Like to Have Heard But Didn't

From my son:
  "*You always know what to say to make me feel better.*"

From my daughter:
  "*I will always love you even though you're imperfect.*"

From my son's teacher:
  "*I wish we had twenty Adams.*"

From my daughter's boyfriend:
  "*Do you think going to Europe together is a good idea? I'd really like to hear your opinion, Mrs. Cohen.*"

From God:

> "There is no way, ever, that you or yours will be hurt, damaged, or lost at sea."

Things I Did Hear That Mattered More Than Anything Else

From my husband:

> "Just do it. You have to do it. No question about it, you can do it. It's not too late."

30

THE RICHLY LAYERED

MARRIAGE

Just when you think you know everything there is to know about him, there's another level revealed. If you dig.

I'm covering a marriage encounter workshop, an intensive two-day deal; we're supposed to bring our partners, so Larry is coming. We're pretty uppity about the whole thing, though, laughing in our beer: what can they teach *us* about marriage? More to the point, Larry has a pretty low tolerance for psychobabble.

I make him promise not to act badly.

The day before the workshop, I switch on Oprah and catch the leader of the forthcoming workshop—a Dr. Harville Hendrix, bespectacled, serious. Then Oprah flashes close-up shots of weeping, troubled couples, and with a major stomach gripe, I think, *Larry's going to hate this.* I fill a tote bag with munchies and prepare. I just hope they let you go to the bathroom on demand.

Hendrix lectures to the assembled group—we're lawyers, doctors, a meat cutter, an historian, an artist, a stockbroker, a spiritual healer—we're everybody.

Marriage is about finishing childhood, he says. We marry people not because the chosen one is handsome, intelligent, kind, or sensitive, but because something deep inside of us recognizes him or her as someone who reminds us of our lost childhood selves. We unconsciously choose people who embody the worst (*and* the best, but mostly the worst) traits of the people who raised us. We pick our beloveds because instinctively we see in the other a chance to heal old wounds, finish childhood.

Listen carefully, says Hendrix.

Inside each of us is a wounded child. We must heal each other's wounds.

Blah, blah, blah, blah. Who believes all this? Not me. Not my pal Larry. *Nothing* about him reminds me of my parents. *Nothing* about me reminds him of Lee and Moe. Wounded—us? No way. So, continues Hendrix, most of us are in unconscious marriages. We react to each other carelessly, unaware of old wounds.

Hendrix gives us exercises to help us find the wounded child in the other. I scribble away, interested but deeply skeptical.

Then Hendrix asks a volunteer couple to demonstrate a certain way of holding each other in a posture designed to break through barriers of communication. He shows the woman how to sit on the floor and cradle her husband in her arms. She is to lean back against the wall so that she can comfortably support his upper body, his face nestled against her chest. Then the husband is to talk to his wife of his feelings about his parents and other frustrations. He is to request specific behavioral changes on his wife's part. Then they are to reverse the position, with the husband holding his wife close as she discusses her own memories and needs.

Piece of cake, Larry and I say. We can do this. We always hold each other, share confidences. We'll play this game, just for fun.

Larry sits on the floor and holds me in his arms. I get the giggles as I obediently begin to tell him stuff—but nothing he hasn't heard before sometime in the last thirty years. Then Hendrix spots us and asks us to slightly shift our position. He's noticed that I am helping Larry to support my weight by leaning my elbow on the floor as he holds me. He wants me to be totally cradled by my husband. I laughingly explain that because I love Larry so much, I feel that I need to take just a bit of my weight off him. I'm saving his back, is what I'm doing.

Hendrix looks at me hard and doesn't buy it.

"Is it possible that's what you did with your parents?" he asks. "Took on the responsibility to save their backs even when you were a child and didn't know the first thing about saving backs?"

I sit up with a start. Of course.

As an only child and one of the sole joys of their troubled marriage, I worried constantly about the pain I could cause my parents by getting lost, hurt, or even being mediocre. I never totally relaxed *into* their care but always "did the right thing" to make them happy.

So I curl into my husband, allowing him to support my

weight completely. And something wild happens. I feel like a baby. I feel safe and nurtured. I feel cradled. It opens my heart—and my mouth. I make connections I never made before. I tell Larry things I've never said in quite the same way. How my father never planned for our financial future—and how that made my mother crazy. How, dear and responsible and affectionate as Larry is, he happens to be pretty lackadaisical about our own financial future—and it makes *me* crazy. How I always felt I'd never be able to completely satisfy my parents—and I worry about the same thing with Larry, even though, in contrast with them, Larry never implied I wasn't satisfying him. Still, there they were—my childhood wounds reentering my adult life.

Then I hold my husband. He's much bigger than I, and I've never before supported all his weight in just this way. It opens his heart—and also his mouth.

Seems that when he was young with rheumatic fever, his mother overprotected him, babied him, made him wild to escape because he felt—well, unmanned. Seems that when I worry loudly about his taking our boat out in iffy weather, it makes him feel, well—unmanned.

He's a super navigator—intellectually I know that. But still I get so scared that I'll lose him. *I cannot bear when Larry's out on the sea without me—and I won't go on the boat unless the weather looks great. Impasse.* My terror, now that I think of it, is very like the terror I felt in childhood that I'd lose my parents if I didn't protect them.

But my fear reminds Larry of being sick and over-protected. His worst childhood feeling—that of being mom-smothered—is realized in my terror. His desire for freedom and independence is thwarted; his physical need for the ocean shortchanged. All that I was doing to him. Unmanning him.

Is it possible, *me*—acting like his *mom?* Has he really unconsciously married someone who personifies her most hurtful behavior? And here I thought he married me just because I'm fabulous.

We have never talked about these feelings in just this way before.

Also, Larry continues, have I ever noticed how impatient I am with him when I feel he's walking too slowly or taking too much time to figure out a household problem? It reminds him of another childhood wound—a ubiquitous fear of failure. It makes him crazy. So could I please try to conquer my irrational fears every time he wants to fish and the weather isn't perfect—and could I please try to *slow down?*

I can. I will try. I will.

He will, also.

I am humbled. So wise-ass am I. I know everything, don't I.

Oh, God, I'm really going to have to be less arrogant.

———

You learn from everything.

Incredibly, I realize that there are intricately rich layers to our marriage we haven't yet begun to touch—even after three decades. Marriage is never finished. It is a fluid, organic thing. Growing.

So many young women and men are searching frantically for the right mate. The real trick seems to be not in finding the right mate, but in *being* the right mate.

One of the words that Hendrix offers to us is Greek—

philia, which means "love between friends." The aim of the conscious marriage is to appear to each other not as a surrogate parent or an enemy, but as a passionate friend.

The Monday evening after the workshop, I take flowers to my own passionate friend, the first time I've ever done that.

"I kept seeing your darling wounded child, all day," I confess.

He grabs me for such a hug.

31

PASSION

Choose passion over romance: Wild,
deep passion rocks the waves.
Romance is a pretty sunset.

Lake and stream devotees think the ocean's a messy thing.
They prefer their boating calm, their angling ruminative. The
fish they catch are more—well, *refined* than saltwater types.
Standing picturesquely in color-coordinated waders in the
middle of quiet streams, baitcasters lift out dainty bass, their
gray stripes so regular they're easily mistaken for finny Turn-
bull and Asser shirts. Gentleman trout swim sportingly into
neat nets. Perch, as qualified for the social set as Brooke
Astor, volunteer themselves as lunch.

   On the other hand, ocean fishermen, boots definitely
not color-coordinated, deal with more fervid denizens of the
deep. Passionate bonito chase dashing mackerel. Amorous
sailfish spread wide their dorsal fins to gather in the surface
baitfish. Virile blues show off their colors. Marlin strut their
stuff. The energy in the air is nuclear. Hot-blooded fishermen
can barely contain their lust. And on wild days, when the
water rolls and the hair blows, a wide, silver-black sky is
gorgeously lit by a shaft of late August light. The fish flail
throbbing, into the boat.

Oh, it's a messy business all right. Ocean angling is to stream fishing as Madonna is to Fred Astaire.

It's the difference between passion and romance.

I thought I knew about passion when I was twenty. I was stuck in the throes of a feeling that was so enormous, so heart-hammering, I thought I'd die of love. I coveted him hopelessly and totally. I watched for the back of his loden green jacket on the college quad, and when I spotted it in a crowd of students, I literally could not breathe. He wooed me with poetry, but he never called when he said he would, and on a trip together he once made me drive 350 miles in the dark just after I'd received my learner's permit: the poet felt like thinking that night, not driving. I was in his thrall, his slave—that's the only way I can put it. I, who had never before made love to a man, existed in a fever of orgiastic bliss from my groin to my imagination. I dreamed we'd make love in his romantic garret and I'd play muse to my passion's passion.

Well, my mother said I couldn't.

The poet should be grateful. I would have killed him, probably with an ax, after living in the garret for twenty minutes, let alone twenty years. I mistook romance for passion.

Do you want to know passion?

Passion is sleeping fitfully on a narrow bunk bed on a rocking boat and waking at dawn to discover that sometime in the night, Larry piled up half a dozen life cushions by my side—God forbid I should fall from my berth. Such a welling up of warmth, I feel. That's passion.

Passion is empathizing with the thrill of a man watching his small child (or anyone else's small child) wind in a prize bluefish from foam-boiled waves. You just love that man.

Passion is taking a Coast Guard boat-maintenance course (you're the only woman in the class amid low-life chauvinists) in order to learn the innards of the accursed engine so when it breaks down midsea, you can be helpful. He so *appreciates* your commitment to his obsession, he falls head over heels in love with you all over again.

Passion is buying a giant boiled lobster from the lobsterman's trawler and, on a gently rocking deck, eating ourselves sick because for the first time in our lives, we have *enough* lobster: when, with his tanned, elegant fingers, he traces the outline of my sun-wrinkled face as if it were a Demi Moore face and says with wonderment, "I love to look at you, I love your mouth," as if he just noticed it for the first time—that's passion.

Passion is playing to each other with loony faces and "little" voices no one else ever saw or heard.

Passion is accepting the other's peculiar spin on things and not being embarrassed when he says an unpopular, redundant, or too revealing thing in public: or better yet, swallowing embarrassment because you love him.

Passion is empowering the other—then feeling stronger yourself.

Passion is loving someone so much you get goose bumps when you know you're about to meet him for dinner. Note, I'm not talking about affection (how great to see you) or romance (I wonder what he's thinking), but passion, *passion* (when can we go home?).

Passion is his hand on my wrist to pull me close, his

eyes smiling. Hello, Wife, he says when he comes in the door. Wife. He makes the word a tiny jewel.

Hello, Husband. Such words.

———

Fitz-Greene Halleck was a nineteenth-century poet who thought you lost it as you aged.

"There is an evening twilight of the heart," he wrote, "when its wild passion-waves are lulled to rest."

Wrong, Halleck. Wild, deep, mutual passion roils the waves even more wildly in the evening twilight. This kind of passion is when you have to hide it from the grown kids: it's too embarrassing.

———

There is something in scientific literature called love blindness, a condition caused by hormonal deficiencies. People who have love blindness can form friendships but are constitutionally unable to fall crazy in love, unable to experience giddy crushes and heartache, unable to feel the *drama* of passion. They cannot experience intense, mutual passion any more than the color-blind can perceive certain hues.

Give me anything, Oh Lord, but love blindness. Give me locusts, hail, darkness, boils—any old plague you can dream up. Only, let me keep passion.

THE SECRETS

1. Reach back into the memory of your first date together and recapture the way you felt. Do it often.

2. Love has only one sure route: unconditional support, even if you're scared, even if you have to bluff it.

3. When you're upset, let the other know—even if you seem crazy.

4. Tend the superstructure of the marriage. Don't let it accumulate dry rot, never aim for its humming heart , cherish its dignity.

5. Spend time together: hearing about catching the shark isn't the same as feeling shark's breath.

6. Create love rituals. Make sure number one is: Always pull socks on the other's cold feet.

7. We become what we name each other. Call me Rascal and watch how cute and rascally I get. Call me Stubborn and watch.

8. See the beauty in what he loves, even if it looks, for a minute, like ground-up fish bait.

9. Speak your love out loud. Saying it often—saying it enough—makes it invincible.

10. Be an island. Sting if the world moves in too close.

11. Hold your horses, bide your time, cool your heels: eventually, the bait looks interesting to the fish.

12. Give some, get some: we take and give back through all our days.

13. The tides are constant, and you better be, too: it's monogamy, honey, or I'm out of here.

14. *Dependency* is not a dirty word. Risking reliance on another can be the way to self-growth.

15. True intimacy requires a dollop of mystery and a tad of Victorian modesty.

16. Lying, even a little, puts you in treacherous water; getting your bearings in marriage requires honesty in the small things.

17. Adventures together whet the marital appetites.

18. Never take the other for granted or push him too far.

19. Home is safe harbor for all the family—even if they kick up a storm there.

20. Try not to try to change him.

21. Can you divert him from a heavy heart? Better learn how.

22. Let the lines out: unravel the knots that choke relationships.

23. A good laugh tames a tempest. If you're not funny, *get* funny.

24. Only when you let yourself be completely vulnerable will the earth move.

25. An occasional change of scenery makes the show come alive!

26. When the other's in trouble, *do* something.

27. When you marry your best friend, the talk never grows old, the sex never grows cold.

28. "Go play," our mothers told us. Who would have thought that playing was the ultimate sex technique?

29. The confidence of a mate is "The Gift of the Magi."

30. Just when you think you know everything there is to know about him, there's another layer revealed. *If* you dig.

31. Choose passion over romance: Wild, deep passion rocks the waves. Romance is a pretty sunset.

FOR THE BEST IN PAPERBACKS, LOOK FO

In every corner of the world, on every subject under the sun, Pengu. quality and variety—the very best in publishing today.

For complete information about books available from Penguin—including Puffins, Penguin Classics, and Arkana—and how to order them, write to us at the appropriate address below. Please note that for copyright reasons the selection of books varies from country to country.

In the United Kingdom: Please write to *Dept. JC, Penguin Books Ltd, FREEPOST, West Drayton, Middlesex UB7 0BR.*

If you have any difficulty in obtaining a title, please send your order with the correct money, plus ten percent for postage and packaging, to *P.O. Box No. 11, West Drayton, Middlesex UB7 0BR*

In the United States: Please write to *Consumer Sales, Penguin USA, P.O. Box 999, Dept. 17109, Bergenfield, New Jersey 07621-0120.* VISA and MasterCard holders call 1-800-253-6476 to order all Penguin titles

In Canada: Please write to *Penguin Books Canada Ltd, 10 Alcorn Avenue, Suite 300, Toronto, Ontario M4V 3B2*

In Australia: Please write to *Penguin Books Australia Ltd, P.O. Box 257, Ringwood, Victoria 3134*

In New Zealand: Please write to *Penguin Books (NZ) Ltd, Private Bag 102902, North Shore Mail Centre, Auckland 10*

In India: Please write to *Penguin Books India Pvt Ltd, 706 Eros Apartments, 56 Nehru Place, New Delhi 110 019*

In the Netherlands: Please write to *Penguin Books Netherlands bv, Postbus 3507, NL-1001 AH Amsterdam*

In Germany: Please write to *Penguin Books Deutschland GmbH, Metzlerstrasse 26, 60594 Frankfurt am Main*

In Spain: Please write to *Penguin Books S. A., Bravo Murillo 19, 1° B, 28015 Madrid*

In Italy: Please write to *Penguin Italia s.r.l., Via Felice Casati 20, I-20124 Milano*

In France: Please write to *Penguin France S. A., 17 rue Lejeune, F-31000 Toulouse*

In Japan: Please write to *Penguin Books Japan, Ishikiribashi Building, 2-5-4, Suido, Bunkyo-ku, Tokyo 112*

In Greece: Please write to *Penguin Hellas Ltd, Dimocritou 3, GR-106 71 Athens*

In South Africa: Please write to *Longman Penguin Southern Africa (Pty) Ltd, Private Bag X08, Bertsham 2013*